MICROEVOLUTION

RANCHI ANTHROPOLOGY SERIES-4

RANCHI ANTHROPOLOGY SERIES

1. Process, Performance, and Pilgrimage: A Study in Comparative Symbology/ Victor Witter Turner
2. Development of Researches in Anthropology in India: Bihar–A Case Study/ L.P. Vidyarthi and V.S. Upadhyay
3. Nature-Man-Spirit Complex in Tribal India/ R.S. Mann and Vijay S. Sahay
4. Microevolution/ B.M. Das
5. Tribal Festivals of Bihar: A Functional Analysis/ Ajit K. Singh
6. The Spectrum of the Sacred: Essays on the Religious Traditions of India/ Baidyanath Saraswati
7. Folklore: The Pulse of the People/ Mazharul Islam
8. Museums, the Public and Anthropology/ Michael M. Ames

About the Author

B.M. Das was educated at Calcutta University (M. Sc., 1953; Ph. D., 1959; D. Sc., 1973). He was an Alexander von Humboldt Fellow and did post-doctoral research in the Institut für Anthropologie, Freie Universität, Berlin (1968-70) and Institut für Genetik, Medizinische Hochschule, Hannover (1975), Federal Republic of Germany.

He was professor and head of the department of anthropology in the Dibrugarh University, Assam (1973-76) and currently is professor and head of the department of anthropology in the Gauhati University, Assam.

He has published a large number of research papers and notes in various journals of India and abroad. Further, he has published ten popular books on anthropological topics in Assamese besides several popular scientific articles in Assamese and English.

Among his published books are *The Ethnic Affinities of the Rabha* (1960); *Kaharpara: A Report on Socio-Cultural Survey* (1964); *Outlines of Physical Anthropology* (1961) Fifth edition (1980); *Anthropometry of the Tribal Groups of Assam, India* (1970); *Variation in Physical Characteristics in the Khasi Population of North East India* (1978); *Contemporary Anthropological Research in North east India* (edited) 1974.

RANCHI ANTHROPOLOGY SERIES-4

Gen. Editor : L.P. VIDYARTHI

MICROEVOLUTION

B.M. DAS

CONCEPT PUBLISHING COMPANY PVT. LTD.
NEW DELHI-110059

ISBN: 978-81-7022-189-0

Edition 2023

Published and Printed by

Concept
Since 1974

Concept Publishing Company Pvt. Ltd.
A/15-16, Commercial Block, Mohan Garden,
New Delhi-110059 (India)
T: 91-11-41101460
E: publishing@conceptpub.com, *W*: www.conceptpub.com

TO

MY TEACHER

DR S.S. SARKAR

GENERAL EDITOR'S INTRODUCTION

IT GIVES us great pleasure to place before our readers the fourth volume under the "Ranchi Anthropology Series". This publication programme launched in 1979 under the U.G.C. Centre of Special Assistance has so far published three distinguished titles: *Process, Performance and Pilgrimage: A Study in Comparative Symbology* (Victor Turner), *Development of Researches in Anthropology in India: Bihar: A Case Study* (Eds. L.P. Vidyarthi and V.S. Upadhyay) and *Nature-Man-Spirit Complex in Tribal India* (Ed. Dr. R.S. Mann). While the first title is based on the lectures of the distinguished anthropologist, Dr Victor Turner delivered at the Centre, the second one is based on a national seminar held on the history and future of anthropology in Bihar in particular and India in general, and the third includes a series of ten papers based on doctoral theses, or large scale reports on the broader theme of anthropological ecology focusing the cross-cultural and cross-regional applicability of the concept of Nature-Man-Spirit Complex described originally in the book, entitled *The Maler: A Study in Nature-Man-Spirit Complex among the Hill tribes of Bihar* (*Vidyarthi*, 1963).

The present volume includes a series of lectures delivered by Professor B.M. Das at the Centre at Ranchi under the U.G.C. Scheme of National Lectureship. These lectures treasured here on the fascinating theme of microevolution were heard and discussed profitably by a sizeable group of researchers, teachers and students drawn from various University Departments and local research institutions. A few outstation specialists including Mr H.K. Rakshit, Director of the Anthropological Survey of India, actively participated in the deliberations which lasted for three days.

I am grateful to Professor Das for having agreed to improve the text in the light of the deliberations and to present the same for publication under the "Ranchi Anthropology Series" in the shortest possible time.

Dr A.K. Dhan, Vice-Chancellor of Ranchi University and a knowledgeable person on the North-Eastern situations, where he also served as Vice-Chancellor at the North-Eastern Hill University, has put us under special obligation by kindly writing a Foreword which has enhanced the value of the book.

I am also grateful to the Publisher, Shri Naurang Rai and his editor Srimati Ramaswamy for ensuring a prompt and flawless publication of this and other titles under this series.

I am sure this publication will fulfil the long felt need of a full-length treatise on Micro-evolution in the Indian context, a study of which was initiated in the sixties by the late Dr S.S. Sarkar.

L.P. VIDYARTHI

FOREWORD

NORTHEAST India is very often described as the paradise for anthropologists because it provides shelter to a large number of populations, who speak various languages, have different socio-cultural heritages and show variation in physical features. And as such, this region attracted the attention of many anthropologists, linguists, ethnologists, travellers, missionaries and administrators of different countries of the world. In view of such an ethnological situation a large number of monographs, ethnographic notes, handbooks and travel accounts have been written by scholars like Gurdon, Playfair, Hutton, Mills and Waddell during the period in the late nineteenth century and the early part of the present century. The rich traditions of these scholars were continued by the British anthropologists particularly Haimendorf and Elwin and American anthropologists like Burling. Their scholarly tradition to study the life and culture of the peoples of this region was carried on by our pioneering Indian anthropologists like K.P. Chattopadhyay, T.C. Das and J.K. Bose.

In the contemporary time several scholars of the Anthropological Survey of India, Departments of Anthropology of the Universities of Gauhati and Dibrugarh and the research wing of NEFA administration headed by Verrier Elwin have published a series of books and papers on the population of this region. Among them Elwin's *A Philosophy for NEFA* is an analytical work on applied nature and has exercised considerable influence on the tribal policy followed by the Government of India specially on Northeastern region.

These works, however, failed to analyse the process and nature of transformation that have taken place among the populations of this region. It is also primarily because of this fact that the contemporary Northeastern situation is characterised with the factors of conflicts, tensions and above all sociopolitical changes. This book of Professor B.M. Das entitled *Microevolution* will perhaps help in some way in understanding the process of fission and fusion in bringing about micro-evolutionary changes that characterize this region.

Among several issues of a basic nature, the book highlights that populations of the same ethnic origin tend to split up into smaller groups because of various factors. Again, for some other reasons, several smaller populations who had their individual identities appear to be heading towards formation of a larger unit. In some regions of Northeastern India certain populations involved in these processes have shown microevolutionary trends, which have been highlighted in the present publication. These processes have been established in the light of case studies done among some of the major ethnic groups like the Boro, Khasi and the Chutia.

I am extremely happy to know that this book has emerged out of his lectures delivered in the Department of Anthropology of this University in August, 1980 under the auspices of the University Grants Commission's National Lecture Programme. I am further pleased to learn that it is being published under the Ranchi Anthropology Series of the UGC Centre of Special Assistance in Anthropology edited by Professor L.P. Vidyarthi. I am sure that this publication will be helpful in clarifying some of the bio-social aspects of Northeast India in particular, and India in general.

A.K. DHAN
Vice-Chancellor,
Ranchi University, Ranchi.

PREFACE

THE University Grants Commission, New Delhi invited me to participate in its Programme of National Lectures during the year 1979-80. Accordingly, a series of lectures on different topics were delivered by me in the universities of Andhra, Karnataka, Punjabi and Ranchi. One of the topics was 'Microevolution'. In Ranchi University after the lectures Professor L.P. Vidyarthi, Head of the Department of Anthropology, Ranchi University suggested to me to develop the lecture on microevolution to the form of a book. I liked his idea. My presidential address at the Anthropology and Archaeology Section of the 66th Indian Science Congress Association held at Hyderabad in 1979 was on the subject 'On some aspects of variation and ongoing human evolution'. The present book is nothing but the enlarged and improved version of these two lectures.

Long back in 1957 my teacher Dr S.S. Sarkar of Calcutta University drew my attention to and since then made me interested in this subject of microevolution. I am always very much indebted to my most revered teacher Dr Sarkar.

Professor Vidyarthi not only suggested the idea but also took the responsibility to get the book published. It is because of him the work has come to the light. I take this opportunity to acknowledge my sincere and deep sense of gratitude to my friend Professor Vidyarthi.

The lectures laid the foundation of the book. Therefore, I am thankful to the University Grants Commission and also to Professor G. Golla Reddy of Andhra University, Professor R.P. Srivastava of Karnataka University, Dr L.S. Sidhu of Punjabi University and Professor L.P. Vidyarthi of Ranchi University for inviting me to their respective departments to deliver lectures.

I am thankful to my colleague Dr Renuka Das, who helped me at different levels at the time of preparing the book and also to Sri Rati Kanta Das, who did the typing and Sri Naba Kumar Choudhury, who prepared the plates and maps. I offer my sincere thanks to all those who directly and indirectly helped me in bringing out this publication. Lastly, I owe an apology to the readers for any error that may have crept into the book.

Department of Anthropology
Gauhati University
Gauhati, Assam, India
15 August 1981

B.M. DAS

CONTENTS

LIST OF PLATES

LIST OF MAPS

INTRODUCTION

Ongoing Human Evolution 1

THE STUDY of human evolution and of human variation are two major focuses of physical anthropology. Human evolution can be viewed from two different angles. Man is a product of the evolutionary processes. Man emerged from some non-human primate stock. It is the task of physical anthropology to trace back that non-human ancestry from which man originated. Man had to pass through various developmental stages to attain his present status, which distinguishes him from other organisms. Therefore, investigation and interpretation of the hominoid and hominid fossil records in order to establish their phylogenetic relationship to understand various stages of human evolution is of great importance to physical anthropologists. In that connection they mostly investigate the gross structural characteristics of man. The present concept of man's ancestry is based on studies of such long-term evolutionary adaptations affecting gross structural changes accomplishing evolution. Of course, at the same time, the study of evolutionary mechanism or the factors influencing evolutionary changes is equally important and interesting, without which the knowledge of human evolution will not be perfect.

From the gross structural and developmental point of view, man has essentially been the same kind of animal over the last thirty thousand years or so. Does it mean that human evolution has come to an end and the evolutionary processes are not functioning? No, it is not. Dealing with the large-scale or long-term evolutionary changes is one aspect of the study, the other aspect being understanding of the short-term evolutionary trends in man at a microlevel, which is an ongoing process. Consideration of physical diversity among the living peoples of the world to understand the ongoing processes on relatively short-term basis at microlevels may be regarded as experimental in anthropological sense.

After all, what is evolution? The development of dissimilarities between the ancestral and the descendant populations may be regarded as evolution. The dissimilarities are in respect of gene frequencies as well as morphological characters. The dissimilarities are caused by change or modification in characteristics through certain processes which may be regarded as evolutionary factors. Hence, first it is necessary to identify the ancestral and descendant populations and then to look at evolutionary aspects.

In recent years the science of genetics has made a rapid progress. The development of genetic knowledge has brought about many remarkable changes in different conceptions in anthropology including the concept of human evolution. From the genetic point of view human evolution may be conceived as occurring through changes in the gene frequency in the gene pool of human population. But in studying human evolution one should not completely ignore the morphological characters. Buettner-Janusch (1969 : 9) has rightly stated that "evolution is also necessarily be viewed as changes in the morphology of organisms through time". Morphological characters include many variables like size, shape, colour of an organism. As a matter of fact in traditional physical anthropology normal morphology constitutes the central field of study. The same is true in the case of Palaeontology and Zoology also.

In the language of Kraus and White (1956) we can say that microevolution is generally "very slight changes in gene frequencies that occur generation by generation in populations of various sizes". Though in the modern genetic concept evolution is nothing but a change in gene frequencies generation by generation, yet as has already been stressed the study of morphological characters and the nature of their changes should not be ignored while dealing with human evolution. No doubt, morphological forms represented by anthropometric measurements and somatoscopic observations are traits of continuous variation and are determined by several loci and hence may be regarded as polygenic, yet as has been stated by

Oliver and Howells (1957) "these traits constitute a whole field of human variation in size and shape, furthermore involving modification by environment as well as the relationship and differentiation of populations—in short, all the processes of microevolution".

Macroevolution and microevolution are basically the same, one does not differ entirely from the other. The study of one helps in understanding the other. Therefore, Dobzhansky (1964 : 17) has clearly stated that "the words 'microevolution' and 'macroevolution' are relative terms, and have only descriptive meaning; they imply no difference in the underlying causal agencies". "Cumulative effect of microevolution through ages leads to macroevolution. An effective breeding population during a certain period of time at a specific level should be taken into consideration to study microevolution".

There was a time when it was believed that human races are unchanging and static. Physical traits distinguishing one ethnic group from another were supposed to be constants. However, in the event of admixture ethnic groups may change assuming new characteristics. For any variation or for any 'intermediate' population hybridization was a common explanation, because of lack of evolutionary concept. In classical anthropology, populations are described in terms of the statistical averages of characters. Franz Boas (1911 *et seq.*) opened a new chapter in physical anthropology by demonstrating the plastic nature of those metric traits causing change in the statistical averages. This may result in the formation of a 'new' population distinguishable from the parental population. Thereby, dissimilarities between the ancestral and the descendant populations may develop.

It was demonstrated by Boas that American-born descendants of immigrants differ in certain physical types from their foreign-born parents. He found changes in head form, face, stature and so on. His study reveals certain important facts. For example, with the change of environment but without change in descent, the form of the head may undergo some modifications. The pattern of the genotype may remain the same, but the expression of the genotype may show changes because of interaction with the changed environment. Another important aspect is that with the lapse of time the influence of environment increases resulting in more modification. Unfortunately, probably Boas's views did not get due recognition until the publication of Shapiro's remarkable work on *Migration and Environment* (1939).

Shapiro in his study of Japanese immigrants into Hawaii found increase and decrease in respect of anthropometric traits. In his study, the Japanese sedents formed the base line, whereas the other two variants were—Japanese immigrants resident in Hawaii and Hawaiian-born Japanese. Of the principally affected characters, mention of the following may be made. The Hawaiian-born males showed significant increments over the immigrants in respect of : stature, sitting height, trunk height, arm length—both upper and lower, leg length—both total and lower, shoulder breadth, head breadth and head height. On the other hand they showed significant decreases in : head length, total facial height, nasal breadth, chest depth and chest width. Then he found significant changes among the Hawaiian-born males in certain proportions like, cephalic index, nasal index, length-height index, shoulder-hip index.

Shapiro noted certain somatoscopic characters also, of which a few traits may be mentioned here. In respect of hair form, he observed an increased tendency towards greater waviness from the sedents to the immigrants and then to the Hawaiian-born. The frequency of coarse hair decreased from the sedents to the immigrants and then finally to the Hawaiian-born. As regards height and slope of forehead, Shapiro observed little differences among the three groups. Both the Hawaiian-born and the immigrants showed greater development of supraorbital ridges than the sedents. Both the Hawaiian-born and the immigrants possessed more medium and high nasal roots and fewer deep nasal roots than the sedents. The percentage of medium lip increased while that of thick lips decreased from the sedents to the Hawaiian-born. The Hawaiian-born possessed more prominent chins than the sedents.

Goldstein (1943) also studied both metric and qualitative traits of the Mexican immigrants in Texas and their American-born children. The sons were taller having longer hand and higher ear index than their Mexican-born parents. But they showed decreases in respect of weight, bizygomatic breadth, nasal height, nasal breadth, nasal index, ear height, ear breadth and ear index.

Goldstein looked at certain qualitative traits also. He found that the American-born sons differed from their Mexican-born fathers showing thicker lips, darker eye colour, less body fat, more medium body build, wavier hair, shallower nasal root, etc.

Laskar (1946) studied the physical characters of Chinese immigrants and American-born Chinese in the eastern United States. He found that the American-born Chinese males showed significant increase over the immigrants in the following traits : stature, sitting height, span, arm length—total, lower and upper, leg length, foot length, hand length, hand breadth, total facial height, upper facial height, facial breadth, nasal height, bi-iliac width and chest width. Significant decreases were observed in chest depth and nasal breadth. Laskar in his study included certain qualitative characters also. He observed changes in texture of hair, prominence of nose, pigmentation of sclera, amount of hair, etc.

Works of similar nature were done by other investigators also (Ito, 1936; Spier, 1929, etc.). In each, metric traits showed increase and decrease suggesting plastic nature of the traits. And thereby the descendant populations showed a tendency to differ from the parental populations. This clearly indicates that a population tends to change in bodily form when it migrates from one geographical area to another. Therefore, if the traits by which a population is described and distinguished are themselves changeable, then how can an ethnic group or a population be static ?

The same is true with regard to change in gene frequencies. Hirszfeld (1919) first demonstrated that ethnic groups differed in their gene frequencies of the ABO blood group genes. Since then more and more informative materials on this subject from among various human populations of the world have been made available for examination. At one time it was thought that blood groups are non-adaptive in nature. But maternal-fetal incompatibility of Rh and ABO blood groups is a very clear evidence for affect of natural selection on the blood groups. In recent years several notable works demonstrating association between blood groups and various types of disease like measles, diptheria, tuberculosis, small pox, typhoid have been published. Now, it is a known fact that the blood groups are not free from the influence of natural selection and their gene frequencies in a population may be altered. Thus, if a change in the gene frequencies of a population is considered as evolution, then evolution is an ongoing process. Population dynamism suggests microevolutionary trends.

The recent development of human genetics has enabled us to know much about such allellic systems in man as the blood groups, haemoglobins and serum proteins. This has helped to investigate into the evolutionary forces acting in the various populations of the present day world. The changes brought about by these forces may be very small in magnitude over a single generation or a few generations in comparison to that which are traceable on the evidences of fossil records.

In modern population genetics change in gene frequencies in human populations are generally explained by four major factors, namely, mutation, natural selection, gene flow and random genetic drift. By these four general factors differences in the frequencies of genes among populations can easily be explained, because any gene is capable of mutation. Again, a gene can also drift or flow, and can be adaptive with its various genotypes to a particular environment.

The raw materials for evolution are provided by mutation, which is the source of all genetic variation. Though mutation is the primary source of creating genetic variabilities, it does not accomplish evolutionary changes. Genetic variation among human populations cannot be explained by mutation alone. Because proper evidences to show that there are qualitative differences of mutation among the human populations are still lacking. Besides, mutation tends to be repetitive in nature.

By applying indirect methods the rate of naturally occurring mutation can be calculated. In general it is said that the rate of such mutation is one in ten thousand to one in a hundred thousand. The number of genes in man is roughly of the same order. Again, some of the mutant genes are lethal genes which cause prenatal death, and thereby these genes are automatically eliminated. Other mutant genes may affect fertility or health of an individual. In such cases also these genes are eliminated in the first generation. Only a few mutant genes are neutral. A few others may cause advantageous biological modifications. The genes of the last category deserve consideration in examining evolutionary processes.

Darwin emphasized the importance of natural selection in evolution. No doubt selection has tremendous implications on evolution. Since the time of Darwin several events of selection have been explored, numerous information have been accumulated, and new ideas have been formulated. It must be admitted that though due emphasis was given on natural selection in understanding evolution, yet uptil recent times natural selection was not considered as a very important factor in producing genetic variability among human populations. The increased knowledge of certain haemoglobin genes, more particularly sickle cell gene, and the demonstrated important role played by natural selection in determining the distribution of such haemoglobin variants, have encouraged scholars to undertake studies to understand natural selection as a cause of human diversity.

In earlier times human diversity with regard to hair form, skin colour and the like were explained by as the results of the effects on those traits exercised by environmental factors in different geographical regions of the globe. Those traits were supposed to have definite adaptive values. This was how it was looked at natural selection to play its role in the formation of the major racial groups. At the next stage, that is after formation of the major racial groups, human diversity was tried to be explained by admixture. Due emphasis was not given on natural selection to account for variation in physical traits among populations.

In a very simple way it could perhaps be said that the survival and reproduction of certain alleles at the expense of contrasting ones is the selection. Through selection multiplication of certain genes are facilitated, while others are gradually eliminated. Thus, the end result of selection is the adaptation of certain alleles to some particular sets of circumstances. This leads us to another phenomenon, that is adaptation. In the language of Hulse (1960 : 64) "adaptation is to be understood simply as the possession or acquisition by a population, of a genetic system resulting in the existence of phenotypic expressions which are favourable to survival and reproduction". Thus, natural selection in man has two broad aspects, it operates through either differential fertility or differential mortality. Therefore, the amount and causes of fertility and mortality is determined by the direction and amount of natural selection operating in any human population. Certain genes may become responsible for producing differential fertility rate among different individuals of a human population. In certain cases some genes may affect the normal sperm, egg or embryonic development, thereby leading to genetic death. In other cases, different members of a population may be affected in various ways including social aspects of behaviour, leading to differential reproduction rates, while some members may not be affected at all.

Looking at from a different angle, natural selection may be considered firstly as the competition between individuals within a single population, and secondly, as the competition between populations. The relative fitness of the genotypes reveals the amount of natural selection within a single population. On the other hand, the amount of the competition between populations is expressed by the average fitness of the populations. In the classical model of population genetics we are more concerned with the first category, that is, intrapopulation competition leading to variation. The competition and differences between populations are to be viewed taking into consideration the ecological aspects of the respective populations. By studying intrapopulation variation we know more about the causes of variation, which may be certain types of disease, genetic background and so forth. But the study of interpopulation variation is more important to look at microevolution as in this case the whole population is involved.

Distribution of gene frequencies among human populations is also affected by gene flow. Gene flows by either migration or admixture. Through migration the genotypes evolved in a geographical area find their way to another population elsewhere. As a result of migration intragroup genetic variability within a population tends to increase, while intergroup variabilities tends to decrease. Mating between different groups of peoples may occasionally take place causing genetic variability in the admixtured groups.

It should be kept in mind that migration of a single individual does not have much effect on the genetic composition of a population. If migration takes place repeatedly or if the migration is of a considerably large scale, then changes in gene frequencies become appreciable. We know that because of such large scale and repeated migration of Europeans to North America, the native American Indians were replaced by the former population. The same is true in the case of Formosa where the natives were replaced by the immigrant Chinese. A similar picture is observed in Australia and Latin America also. At a microlevel also people from one small geographical area may move to certain neighbouring areas causing genetic variability in the populations concerned.

Even at a time when notion about race was unscientific and races were regarded as static units, then also admixture or hybridization was recognised as a potent factor for formation of new racial groups. Admixture has been going on since long past. It is taking place in different degrees in different populations giving rise to populations of varied genetic composition. The populations like the Mullatoes, Bastards, Anglo-Indians have been formed by this process.

Random genetic drift is nothing but more accidents of sampling which cause genetic diversity among human populations. This becomes more effective when the population concerned is small in size and remains in complete isolation. As a result of genetic drift non-adaptive, neutral characters or even slightly unfavourable traits may be established in a population. Thus, traits without any adaptive significance may also be the characteristics of a small group. Evidences of random genetic drift in human populations are there in the form of divergent frequencies of specific genes. This is seen in small populations of religious groups, which are endogamous, in isolated hunting or gathering tribal populations and also in small populations living in isolated small islands. For example, in one group of the aborigines of the Wellesley Islands in the Gulf of Carpentaria in Australia, the frequency of blood group A is very high, but B is absent. On the other hand, in another group there is no A, but B is appreciably higher than in any other known population of Australian aborigines. The occurrence of such blood groups in the two populations cannot be explained by any meaningful association between blood group genes and natural selection. This is because of random genetic drift.

In the process of ongoing human evolution mutation, natural selection, gene flow and genetic drift play their respective roles in different degrees and in different ways depending on the circumstances. To understand the matrix of forces anthropologists are to investigate the history, environmental situations, population, structure, mating patterns along with blood group systems, biochemistry and other biological variables of the populations concerned.

Man is a social animal having culture and thereby he is distinguishable from other animals. The evolution of such a highly social species cannot be fully understood without the knowledge of its cultural behaviour and social organization. Human evolution should not be understood as a purely biological process. Biology and culture are two component parts of human evolution. The interaction between the two determines the course of evolution. The interdependence of the two components serve the same basic purpose, that is adaptation to and control of man's environment.

The influence of social life on the trend of human evolution is of such importance that without referring to the socio-cultural behaviour of a population or the human species as a whole human biology is incomprehensible. Socio-cultural variables like linguistic, religious, national, occupational are playing their respective roles in the evolutionary processes of the human populations. For example, the marriage regulations prescribed by different societies according to their social norms have sometimes considerable implications on the occurrence and maintenance of gene frequencies in population groups.

Earlier we referred to gene flow, a progress in which migration, admixture and isolation are involved. Demographic variables like population size, expansion rate and density, may directly be connected with gene flow. Again population size to some extent determines the amount of genetic drift. All these variables are culture-linked. Thus, the role of culture can not be ignored.

Natural selection may also be linked up with the socio-cultural activities of human populations. The rate of mortality and that of fertility are in many cases determined to a considerable extent by socio-cultural differences among populations. Infanticide, death due to accidents and warfare are directly associated with cultural activities. Again, one or the other of certain diseases like measles, small pox, influenza, malaria becomes more effective when the population size is large. And huge host population is the outcome of the agricultural and industrial activities of man.

A classic example of natural selection in man is haemoglobin variants, more particularly Haemoglobin S and Haemoglobin E. This natural selection for these two abnormal haemoglobin is determined by the presence of holoendemic malaria. This type of malaria is in turn associated with a sedentary way of life. Again for such sedentary life agriculture appears to be a prerequisite in most environment. Further, the spread of these two abnormal haemoglobin genes are associated with the spread of agriculture. Let us look at tropical Asia considering the view of Livingstone (1964). Agriculture spread to tropical regions of Asia from two centres, namely, the Middle East and China. The spread of haemoglobin S gene is associated with the spread of agriculture from the Middle East to peninsular India and Africa. On the other hand, haemoglobin E gene penetrated to Indonesia through Southeast Asia along with the spread of agriculture from China.

Cultural evolution is still going on, it is a continuous process, so is the human evolution. Culture and biology are closely interrelated. Culture is spread through society and biology through genes. Man is moulding his culture, he is developing new ways of social life, and at the same time his culture and society are influencing the patterns of his biological evolution.

It has already been mentioned that ecological changes bring about variation in physical features. Such variation was observed by Sarkar (1935-36, 1960), among the Mālés of the Rajmahal Hills. The Mālés form a Veddid population. They gave rise to two new populations—one, the Malpaharias and the other the Plains Mālés. After the Mālé rising in 1772, the British Government induced some of the hill people to settle down in the plains. They were provided with incentives to do so by giving cash and other facilities. Their descendants are the present day Malpaharias. Again, a section of the Hill Mālés on their own came down to settle in the plains. They are called Plains Mālés. This section is not only retaining their original name Mālé, but also their own culture and language. They had undergone admixture to some extent with the low caste Hindu people.

The Hill Mālés show variation in respect of certain metric traits from the Plains Males as well as the Malpaharias. Sarkar observed that "the Plains Males show an increase in stature, head length, head breadth and total facial height, while in the case of the Malpaharias head height, head breadth, minimum frontal breadth and nasal breadth show a tendency to decrease" (Table 1.1). Sarkar's opinion that "a change in habitat, like that from the hills to the plains, or the branching out from the tribal stage amidst other peoples", may cause changes in physical features. He further observed that the mating system of the two groups has to some extent undergone change, and this coupled with their population sizes and the opportunities of gene exchange consequent to them. Thus

TABLE 1.1 : **Mean values (in cm.) showing INCREASE (+) and DECREASE (—) from hill section to the plain section**

Measurements	Hill Males	Plains Males	Hill Garos	Plains Garos
Stature	156.64	158.11 +	159.49	161.92 +
Head length	18.42	18.45 +	18.79	18.72 —
Head breadth	13.72	13.77 +	14.10	14.19 +
Head height	13.35	13.13 –	12.01	12.06 +
Frontal breadth	10.05	10.01 –	10.62	10.48 –
Bizygomatic breadth	13.09	13.02 –	13.87	13.77 —
Bigonial breadth	9.68	9.44 –	10.10	10.08 –
Nasal height	4.72	4.59 –	4.69	4.78 +
Nasal breadth	3.96	3.87 –	4.00	3.94 —
Upper facial height	6.56	6.38 –	6.70	6.59 —
Total facial height	10.96	11.00 +	11.34	11.44 +

the whole process is culturally conditioned. Therefore, according to Sarkar "herein comes the joint field of work or the physical and the cultural anthropologist". Such environmental changes in physical features may be regarded as process of microevolution.

A similar phenomenon was observed by the present writer (Das, 1960) among the Garo tribe. Though the Garos are essentially a hill people, a section of them moved to the plains to settle there permanently and as a result at present according to their habitat two distinct sections of the Garos are met with—the Hill section and the Plains section. However, it can not be said that the two sections are completely separated forming two different tribal groups. But for various socio-cultural and geographical reasons the members of each one prefer to marry within the section.

It was found that the Plains Garos were significantly taller than the Hill Garos. Their face and nose were longer and narrower. Though both had long, narrow head, the Plains Garos appeared to show a slight inclination towards rounder head. Thus in certain traits the Plains Garos showed an increase, while in others a decrease (Table 1.1).

Oliver and Howells (1957) while dealing with cultural elements in physical variation in directing microevolutionary trends also suggested that "cultural and physical anthropologists might profitably exploit such inquiries more fully". They found two neighbouring populations, Nagovisi and Siuai, in the Melanesian island of Bougainville separated for more than two centuries now differing from each other although they appear to show a common origin. Both are mountain dwellers—the Nagovisi living on a higher altitude than the Siuai, who have extended to the plains as well. In physical features the Siuai are consistently larger in size than the Nagovisi except in head, face and jaw breadth. The authors remark: "we can suggest no explanation for this from the data; dietary factors are an obvious possibility and anthropologists might once have jumped to conclusions about the more mountainous habitat of Nagovisi having an effect". They also point out: "we would have to know a great deal more about (i) specific environmental and dietary factors and (ii) the way in which different measured traits respond to environmental influence".

Kraus and White (1956) also stressed on the need for combining the interests and techniques of both physical and social anthropology in studying microevolution in a human population. The title of their work itself implies the emphasis given on the study of social endogamy in dealing with blood type distribution while looking at a case of microevolution. They studied a population of the Fort Apache Indian Reservation in east-central Arizona. They dealt with gene frequencies of ABO, Rh and MN blood types.

As early as 1949, Sanghvi and Khanolkar put due emphasis on the necessity of accurate quantified social data in studying six different endogamous groups of Bombay. The genetic and marriage data of Ramah Navaho were meaningfully analysed by Spuhler and Kluckhohn (1953).

Basu *et al* (1976) studied microevolution of some village populations in Haiti, West Indies with a purpose 'to investigate the effects of social-historical factors on genetic composition'. The analyses of the data confirm their hypothesis of major similarities of the Haitians of African Negroes and the lesser influence of White and Indian elements. They conclude that "while racial admixture and gene flow are evidently the major factors responsible for the general genetic pattern seen in this rural Haitian population, sample size and genetic drift undoubtedly produced some of the variations among individual villages". Their study is based on morphological (anthropometric), serological and dermatoglyphic materials collected from among the populations.

The microevolutionary dynamics among the Gaudas of Goa was studied by Malhotra (1978). He took into consideration thirteen somatometric characteristics, thirteen visual observations, eight genetic traits and also dermatoglyphic traits.

The ongoing microevolutionary trends could be demonstrated better when the population involved in the process is small and Mendelian in nature. A Mendelian population has been defined by Dobzhansky (1964 : 15) as "a reproductive community of individuals which share a common gene pool". A tribe or a case, the member of which are bound together by a network of marriages and of common descent may be called a Mendelian population. In a Mendelian population the gene frequencies tend to remain constant from generation to generation according to Hardy-Weinberg Law. However, this law holds good only when certain conditions are fulfilled. Firstly, genes should not change frequently by mutation. Secondly, there should not be flow of genes from or to the population bringing in or removing gene in preference to the other. Then, there should not be any selective or adaptive forces working, so that the same number of offsprings are survived in the next generation. Again, the population should adequately be large so that accidental fluctuation of gene frequency does not affect the whole population. But in practice only a few populations, perhaps none, fulfil all these conditions strictly. And therefore, there are enormous possibilities of change in such Mendelian populations. Thus, "Mendelian populations have a temporal continuity; they exist through time" (Wallace & Dobzhansky, 1967 : 22).

Certain conditions under which populations are met with are desirable for ideal experimental studies on microevolution. Oliver and Howells (1957) have listed some such required conditions. The list includes knowledge of the genetic stock, relative isolation, subdivision into a kind of block design, some knowledge of factors involved and a culturally caused differentiation in breeding behaviour.

Northeast India is the homeland of a large number of tribes, which in a very broad sense belong to the common ethnic stock, the Indo-Mongoloid. These different tribes entered into this region at different intervals of time and by various routes. Now they are settled in different parts of the region. Each tribe has its own socio-cultural tradition including dialect by which one is distinguishable from the other. But even then the tribes of Northeast India may conveniently be grouped under certain broad headings like the Boro, the Khasi, the Naga, the Lushai-Kuki, the Arunachal tribes and others, the basis of these groupings is the one or the other factor like linguistic affinity, cultural similarity and common territory.

The Khasis live in the state of Meghalaya, while Nagaland is the habitat of the Nagas, though they are met with in the adjoining territories. The Lushai-Kuki tribes are found in Mizoram as well as some adjoining regions. Arunachal Pradesh provides shelter to a large number of tribes, of which mention may be made of Monpa, Sherdukpen, Aka, Nishi, Apatani,

Tagin, Adi, Singpho, Khamti, Mishimi, etc. The term Boro is used to denote a large number of peoples who speak Boro languages, and thus there is a common linguistic affinity among the different members of this group. The Boro, not at a very distant past, proved themselves to be a very powerful people occupying almost the entire Brahmaputra valley. They even extended their area of occupation to northern Bengal. To the south they not only occupied the Garo Hills, the abode of the Garos, who are a Boro-speaking tribe, but also spread to northern Maimanshing (now in Bangladesh). From Nowgong district of Assam their territory extended to North Cachar and into Sylhet (now in Bangladesh). From these places again they extended further south to Tripura. Hence, they are distributed over a very large area.

Thus, Northeast India being the homeland of numerous populations of various ethnic origins having different cultural heritages and social structures, and living in different degrees of isolation and in different stages of culture change provides ample scope for such anthropological researches to look at microevolutionary trends. Now, we propose to refer to a few case studies of microevolutionary trends done among certain populations of Northeast India.

Microevolutionary Trend in the Boro Populations* 2

THE SOUTH bank of the Goalpara district of Assam is a narrow strip of land covering an area of about 1275 square miles and is bounded by the northern part of the Garo Hills of the Meghalaya state in the south, the Brahmaputra river in the north and west, and the Kamrup district in the east (Map No. 1). South Goalpara is a plain land as far as the valley of the Brahmaputra extends, beyond which the region is hilly. Small and low ranges of the Garo Hills are, however, seen towards the southern edge of the valley with jungle here and there. A few ranges reach right into the Brahmaputra river near Goalpara town. Besides these ranges, a number of small isolated hillocks with the height varying between about 125 to 225 metres above the alluvial plains have made some parts undulating. The bank of the Brahmaputra is more or less flat and low compared to the southern border of the district.

The geographical region under consideration is inhabited mostly by a few Mongoloid populations, Assamese Hindu castes and Muslims. In the present context we are concerned with four Mongoloid populations, namely, the Garo, Rabha, Kachari and Rajbanshi. The first three are tribes. After independence of India tremendous changes have occurred in the socio-cultural life of the tribal populations of many parts of North-east India. Without referring to the changing patterns, let us have some general idea about the traditional Garo, Rabha and Kachari.

*The work is based on the present author's Ph.D. Thesis of Calcutta University (1959) entitled Somatic Variability among some Populations of South Goalpara, Assam. The summary was published in the *Proceedings of the National Institute of Sciences of India*, Vol. 30 B, Nos. 5 4 6, 1964, 315-338.

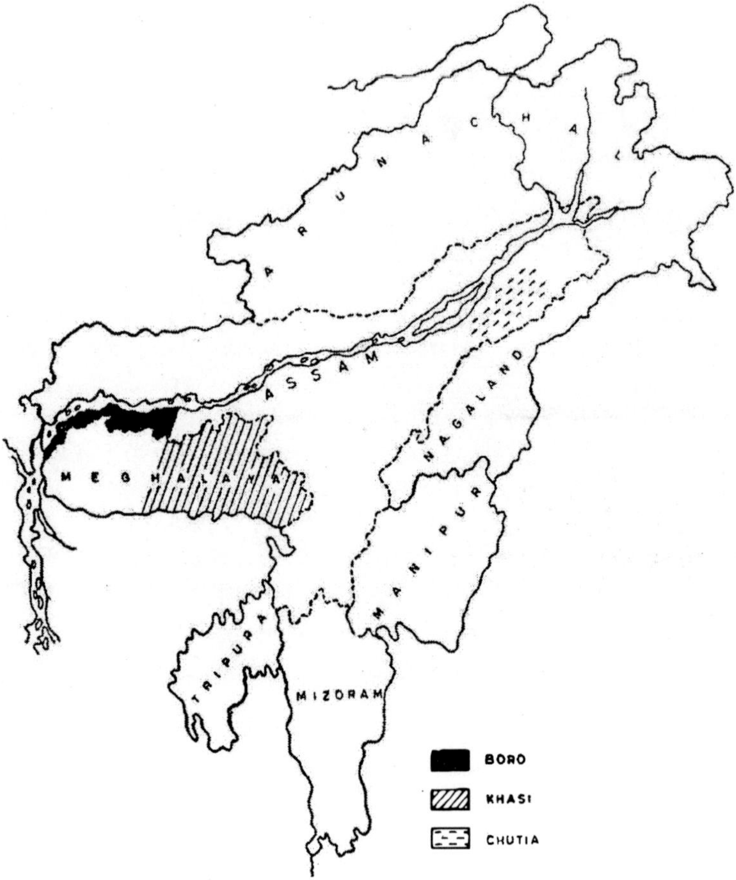

Map 1: Sketch Map of North-East India

Garo

The Garos are essentially a hill people. They mostly live in the Garo Hills of Meghalaya state. However, they have extended their territory to the plains of Goalpara and Kamrup district of Assam adjoining the Garo hills. In the present study we are concerned with the Hill Garos.

Traditionally the Garos practise shifting cultivation. Even today the sole means of subsistence of some sections of the Garos is this type of cultivation. In the jhum fields they grow their principal food crops, rice and millet along with a num-

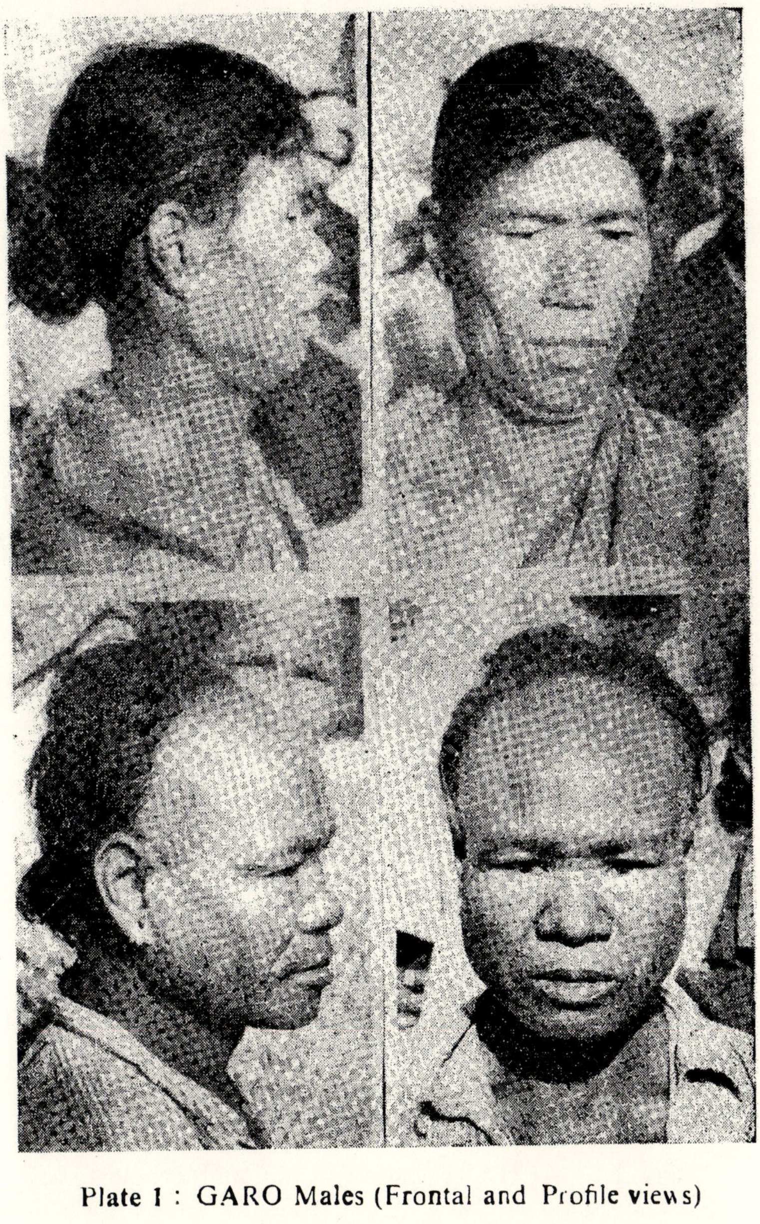

Plate 1 : GARO Males (Frontal and Profile views)

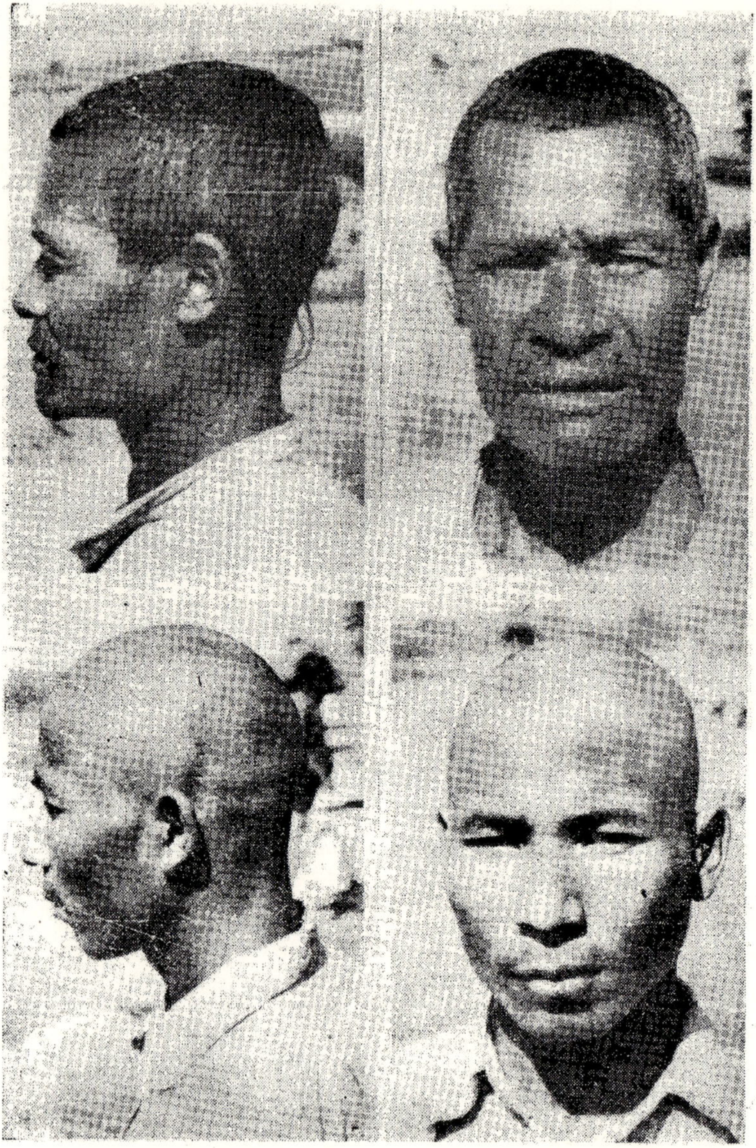

Plate 2 : KACHARI Males (Frontal and Profile views)

ber of subsidiary crops like maize, arum, yam, pumpkin, gourd, chillies, jute, cotton and ginger are also grown in some places, and these are cash crops.

The staple food of the Garos is rice. In addition they also eat millet and maize. The Garos usually take two meals a day. The meal consists of boiled rice and a curry consisting of chillies, vegetable and dry meat or fish. They eat almost all kinds of animal food. Beef is not prohibited to them. Home brewed beer prepared from rice or millet is their common drink. Tobacco is grown by each household. Dried tobacco is smoked after rolling in dried maize seaths.

The Garos establish their villages usually on the slopes of hills or valleys, close to running water. A Garo village usually comprises 20 to 30 households. The Garos build their houses on piles. Split bamboo is used for the floor as well as for the walls. The material for the roof is thatching grass or bamboo leaves.

The Garo society is characterized by matriliny. They trace their descent through the mother. Property is inherited in the female line. However, a female is not regarded as the absolute owner of property, because she cannot dispose it at her will. She is to consult her husband who acts as the manager of property. One of the daughter is selected by the parents to be the inheritress, who is known as Nokna. Her husband is called Nokrom, who should preferably be her father's sister's son. A Nokrom usually lives in the household of his wife's father, on whose death he takes over as the head of the household. A son-in-law, who is not a Nokma usually establish his household in the village of his wife.

The Garo society consists of five exgamous groups or clans, each again divided into many sub clans known as Maharies, related on the mother's side. A Garo family includes a married couple, their unmarried children and a married daughter (Nokna), her husband and her unmarried children.

Rabha

The Rabhas constitute one of the important plains tribe of Assam. They are mostly met with in the district of Kamrup, Goalpara and Darrang of Assam, but their main concentration is in the south bank of the Brahmaputra river in the Goalpara district.

Agriculture is the main occupation and economy of the Rabhas. Agriculture is practised with the help of plough. Both winter and summer varieties of paddy are cultivated by them. Besides, they grow pulse, sugarcane, tobacco, jute, etc. Cattle, pigs, goats, fowls, dogs, etc., are the major domesticated animals. Cows are not milked, because they do not take milk.

Rice forms the staple food of the Rabhas. Vegetables, pulses, etc. are taken with rice. Dried fish is a delicacy and forms an important article of diet. Beef is prohibited. Rice-beer is their favourite drink.

The Rabha is a plains tribe and their villages are situated on the plains. But in south Goalpara some of them prefer to live in the small hillocks. In lay out a Rabha village is more or less similar to that of an ordinary non-tribal Assamese village of lower Assam. In a village a family owns usually four huts, arranged on the four sides of a courtyard. But in south Goalpara some villages resemble Garo village, though houses are not of pile dwelling type.

The Rabha tribe is divided in several groups, namely, Pati, Maitori, Rangdani, Totla, Bitlia, Dahuri, Shonga, etc., of which the first three constitute the major bulk of the Rabha population. Each group again consists of several exogamous clans, termed as Bar or Barai. Two or more bars may unite to form a lineage called Hur or Huri. Hur is also exogamous.

The bar is matrilineal. But among the Rabhas residence is patrilocal. The father is the head of the family. He is the owner of the property. It appears that the Rabhas are in transition from matriarchy to patriarchy.

Cross cousin marriage is allowed by the Rabhas. In some places it is the preferential one. The Rabhas consider themselves superior to the Garos, and hence no intermarriage between the two is allowed. But intermarriage with the Kacharis is not prohibited. However, a Rabha man may marry a Kachari girl on payment of some fine. After marriage the couple has to pass through a purification ceremony and then she is admitted to the Rabha society.

Kachari

The Kacharis are distributed throughout the entire valley of the Brahmaputra and also in North Cachar hill district of Assam. The tribe has several subdivisions like Thengal, Jharwa, Sonowal, Dimasha. The first three divisions are met with in the Upper Assam districts. The Kacharis of Lower Assam districts are very often referred to as the Boro Kachari. The Dimasha Kacharis are a hill people and they mostly live in the North Cachar hill districts. Here we are concerned with the Kacharis of South Goalpara.

In South Goalpara the Kachari villages are situated in the plains. The huts in the household and the lay out of the village are more or less similar to those of the Rabhas of the plains of South Goalpara. The economic pursuits, food habits, etc., of the Kacharis are also comparable to those of the Rabhas.

The Kacharis are patriarchal people. Unlike the Garos and the Rabhas, the descent among the Kacharis is also patrilineal.

There is no historical record as regard the origin and migration of the Garos. But there is a legend in verse as well as in prose, narrating the story of their migration, on the basis of which, Playfair (1909) has very ably and elaborately dealt with the migratory routes of the Garos from their ancestral place, Tibet to their present homeland, the Garo hills.

Instead of going into the details given by Playfair, very broadly it can be said that the ancestors of the Garos, according to the legend inhabited Torua, a province in Tibet, from where under the leadership of two chiefs they migrated southward to arrive at Rangamati, a place in the plains of northern part of the Goalpara district. Then they moved to further south to reach Dhubri, the present day headquarters of the Goalpara district. Though the local king was friendly to them, yet he did not allow them to settle permanently in his territory. Hence, they moved eastward following the northern bank of the Brahmaputra to reach its affluent the Manas river. There they had to encounter with the local chief, who defeated them. Anyway, eventually near Jogighopa they managed to cross to the Brahmaputra and arrived at the southern bank, that is, south Goalpara. Somewhere there a local chief named

Arambit married a girl of that group, that is, the progenitors of the Garo. At a later date with the permission of Arambit, they established their settlement on Baghmela Pahar, a hill situated at a distance of eight kilometres towards southwest of Boko, a place in the district of Kamrup. From there again they moved towards west. Finally, the group broke up into different branches each moving to different places.

Since long past the legend has passed orally from generation to generation and as such there have been many changes in the names of the places and persons and also the circumstances under which the people had to move resulting in many discrepancies. Even then the legend gives some idea about the migration of the Garos.

Playfair rightly looked at certain cultural elements of the Garos to suggest that those elements "owe their origin to the land form which they claim to have come". For example, Yak, an animal which has remarkable position in the tradition of the Garos, has never been seen by them, Yak's tail plays an important role in their traditional socio-cultural life. To this may be added the gongs which are in the possession of the Garos and are used on several occasions.

In this connection it is to be mentioned that the above mentioned three tribes, the Garo, Rabha and Kachari, belong to a bigger group termed as the Boro, the members of which speak Boro languages of the Tibeto-Burman linguistic group. Besides these three, on the basis of linguistic affinity, Grierson has put some other populations like Mech, Lalung, Dimasa, Tipperah, Moran and Chutia also in the same group. While considering the affinities of the Garos, Playfair has dealt with some of these populations as well. He has given an interesting account regarding the migration of the Boro group, especially of the Kachari, Rabha, Garo and Koch. But as has already been mentioned earlier we are primarily concerned with the Garo, Rabha and Kachari.

There are so many resemblances between the Garo and the Kachari that Playfair thinks that 'the two tribes were originally one and the same'. To establish this fact he has referred to the possible way of their bifurcation, their migration to different regions, their distribution in the contiguous regions, resemblance between the two in respect of certain cultural elements, language and so forth. A Garo legend claims that the Kacharis are the descendants of a Garo girl named Kingsari-Kangsari, who married a non-Garo, when the Garos were residing at Jogighopa.

Some legends are prevalent among the Rabhas also. According to one, a section of the Rabhas, known as Rangdania Rabhas lived in the Garo hills along with the Garos. They had a series of conflict with the Garos. Finally the Rabhas were driven down to the plains which they now occupy. Another legend narrates that the ancestors of the Rangdani Rabhas and the Atongs, a section of the Garos dwelt in the valley of the Someswari river in the Garo hills. Among their ancestors there were two sisters, named Sae Bonge and Bonge Kate—The descendants of Sae Bonge are the Atong Garos. Bonge Kate had a liaison with her own brother. The guilty couple was driven away by their peoples. The descendants of that couple are the Rangdani Rabhas.

A story about Dadan, a very powerful king of the Rabha tribe, narrated to the present writer by many Rabha individuals was included in one of his books (Das, 1960). The story reveals the migration of the Rabha. It suggests that the ancestors of the Rabha tribe moved from the sub-Himalayan region, north of lower Assam, towards the Brahmaputra valley via Doangiri, through northern Kamrup to arrive at Bakbua hill near Barpeta. There they took rest for a while, then proceeding along the bank of the river Choulkhowa entered the Goalpara district. Near Jogighopa they crossed the Brahmaputra and reached Pancharatna. The party spent a brief period there after which it moved southward along the bank of a rivulet, named Daldunga and ultimately reached Dubu hill near Lakhipur in the Goalpara district.

There are so many similarities with regard to socio-cultural element, language, etc., in between the Garos and the Rabhas that there are reasons to believe that the two tribes originated from the same source. The resemblances between the Rabhas and the Kacharis are also remarkable to suggest to their common origin.

The purpose of including the legends and referring to the resemblances among these three tribes in the present work is to establish the fact that the ancestors of the Garo, Rabha and Kachari were originally one and the same. However, it is difficult to ascertain the time of migration of the ancestors of these peoples and the time of their split into different groups.

Rajbanshi

The Rajbanshis have been recognized as a backward class by the Government. But they themselves claim to be "an outlying branch of the Kshatriyas" (Risley, 1915). They have been described by Allen (1905) as one of the "racecastes" of Assam. To him they appear to be of recent "mixed-lineage".

The Rajbanshis are widely distributed in most of the districts of Assam, the heavicst aggregation being in the valley of the Brahmaputra of the Goalpara district. They are common in North Bengal and Bangladesh also. The North Bengal and Bangladeshi Rajbanshis have been identified as the representatives of the "Dravidian stock who, being driven by pressure from the west into the swamps and forests of Northern and North-Eastern Bengal (now Bangladesh), were brought into contact with the Mongoloid races of the lower Himalayas and the Assam border" (Risley). Waddell (1901) describes them as "distinctly Mongoloid though somewhat heterogeneous". According to Dalton (1872) "they belong to the Dravidian stock, and are probably a branch of the great Bhuiya family". In Census Report of 1881 it is mentioned that "a large number of Koch in the Goalpara district call themselves Rajbanshi", whereas in Census Report of 1891 it is stated that "in Assam the Rajbanshis are mainly persons of the Koch and Mech tribes who have assumed this name on conversion to Hinduism".

Thus, opinions differ as regards the origin and ethnic position of the Rajbanshis. This is, however, true for the Rajbanshis in general. But the situation in south Goalpara, wherefrom the sample included in the present study comes, gives a slightly different picture. In south Goalpara peoples of different tribal groups (it should be kept in mind that the tribes of south Goalpara are mostly Garo, Rabha and Kachari) are known as Rajbanshi after conversion to Hinduism, and are given a place in the castefold of the Hindu society. It is not definitely known when this process of conversion commenced, but it appears to be a live process even now and new members are thus being added to the Rajbanshi. Some of the Rajbanshis adopted Hinduism a few generations ago, while others were converted in an undatable past. The latter usually claim that they are pure Rajbanshi and are not the product of any converted tribals. They have no dialect of their own, but speak Assamese.

Considering the ecotypes these four populations of this region can be divided into three ecological categories. First of all, the Garos, who live in the hills, are a hill people. Though a section of them has moved to settle in the plains and hence this section may by regarded as plains Garo, yet the Garos are essentially a hill tribe. On the other hand, the Rajbanshis and Kacharis inhabit the plains region in the river valleys and they are regarded as plains people. Again, the Rabhas occupy a place in between these two categories. The Rabhas are divided into certain subdivisions each having its own name. A subdivision of the Rabhas prefer to establish their villages on the small hillocks and at the foot hills. Thus, the habitat of the Rabhas can be regarded as forming the third ecotype, an intermediate one between the two extremes, hills of the Garos and plains of the Rajbanshis and Kacharis.

The process of detribalization is obvious in many parts of India, particularly where tribes are met with in various transitional phases of culture. This process is very much apparent among these four populations of this small geographical region. Looking at from this point of view the four populations may be grouped under three stages. Firstly, the Garos living in a circumscribed territory of their own, have to a great extent preserved their tribal tradition, though impact of Christianity and modern civilization have brought about many perceptible changes in their way of life. They have their own dialect. The Garos may be considered as a homogenous group in a broad sense. The tribal solidarity based on matriarchy is strongly observed by the Garos.

With regard to the process of detribalization the Rabhas and Kacharis appear to be at the same stage of transition. It should be noted that while the Garos are becoming Christian, the Rabha-Kacharis are being Hinduised. Hinduism has brought about enormous changes in their habits, manners and customs. The Rabhas and Kacharis have their own respective dialects, but they speak Assamese also. One section of the Rabhas has abandoned their own respective dialects, but they speak Assamese also. One section of the Rabhas has abandoned their own dialect in favour of Assamese.

The Rajbanshis appear to represent the end-product of the process of detribalization. The Rajbanshis are of mixed origin in the sense that peoples of different tribal groups after conversion to Hinduism are called Rajbanshi (or Koch). It is very clear that the Rajbanshis constitute a detribalized group which has been forged out of the various tribal societies and now form an integrated part of the Assamese castes.

The Garos are a matriarchal people in the truest sense. They have their own distinctive s ystem of regularization of marriage. The Rabhas appear to be in transition from matriarchy to patriarchy. A Rabha clan is matrilineal, the children take their clan name after the mother. The Kacharis are patriarchal people. Intermarriages between the Rabhas and Kacharis are not infrequent, though it is allowed on payment of some fines. The Rabhas are divided into several groups, of which the Pati, Rongdani and Maitari constitute the majority of the Rabha population. In one of his work, these three sections of the Rabha were separately studied by the present writer (Das, 1960). But as there are no significant differences among these three sections, here they are pooled together and considered as one population, the Rabha.

It has already been mentioned that these three tribes, viz., the Garo, Rabha and Kachari belong to a bigger stock—the Boro. It has also been stated that the Rajbanshis are of tribal origin. The Rajbanshis of south Goalpara are of Garo-Rabha-Kachari origin and hence may be regarded as one member of the Bodo, not linguistically, but ethnically. As a matter of fact the differences in the constitution of an average Rajbanshi and an average Garo are though obvious to any casual observer, yet the differences do not tempt the observer to put them into two different ethnic groups.

Under these circumstances perhaps we can consider these four populations belonging to one bigger group, now each one having its own identity and each one being endogamous. Traditional stories prevalent in the area tell about the original relationship between the Garo and Rabha.

Now let us examine the physical feature of these four populations from the point of view of microevolution. For that purpose, because of the above mentioned facts, we have taken the Garos as forming the base-line. The Rajbanshis have already been referred to as the end-product of detribalization. Now let us see how far an end-product like the Rajbanshis is supported by data on physical anthropology; and whether any other peplle like the Rabha and Kachari can be associated in the transitional phase—a phase commencing with the Garo and ending into the Rajbanshi.

The following categories of physical characters have been taken into account in the present study: somatoscopic observations, anthropometric measurements, dermatoglyphic traits, ABO blood groups and Rh-factor. We will consider them one by one. The sample of each of the Garo, Kachari and Rajbanshi comprises 100 male persons while that of the Rabha 300 male persons, because of the reason mentioned above. This is in case of somatoscopy and anthropometry. As regards other traits the sample sizes have been shown in respective tables. The abbreviation used for the populations are : G=Garo; Rh=Rabha; K=Kachari; Rj=Rajbanshi.

Somatoscopic observations :

A few characteristics of head hair, beard and moustache, forehead, eye, nose, face, lip, earlobe attachment and body and limbs will be examined. The percentile occurrences of these characteristics have been included to indicate the trend of variation.

Head Hair : The percentage of smooth form of head hair has decreased from the Garo to the Rajbanshi through the Rabha and Kachari. Conversely, the percentage of wavy (flat+broad and narrow) form of hair has increased in the same sequence. In this connection it may be mentioned that broad and narrow wavy hair occurs more frequently among the Rajbanshis (29%) than among the Kacharis (20%), Rabhas (18%) and Garos (21%). Coarse texture of hair is very much less frequent among the Rajbanshis than among the other three.

Smooth hair form		Wavy hair form		Coarse hair texture	
G	60	Rj	56	Rh	94
K	56	Rh	49	G	86
Rh	51	K	44	K	68
Rj	44	G	40	Rj	35

Beard and Moustache : Beard and moustache are scanty in growth in almost in all the subjects belonging to the Garo and Rabha. The same is the case with the Kachari also to some extent. But only one-third of the Rajbanshis have scanty growth of beard and moustache.

G	94
Rh	92
K	85
Rj	33

Forehead : Unlike head hair and beard and moustache in the case of forehead no definite trend of variation is indicated by the percentile occurrence of the different types.

Medium height		Medium breadth		Straight slope		Medium slope		Moderate Suporbital ridge	
K	70	G	77	K	69	G	35	G	64
Rh	69	K	62	Rh	66	Rj	32	Rj	32
G	64	Rj	54	Rj	58	Rh	31	R	29
Rj	54	Rh	29	G	49	K	21	Rh	9

Eye : Oblique slits occur less frequently in the Rajbanshis than in the other three populations. In case of palpebral fissure though the variation among the populations does not show any distinct trend, it is clear that narrow palpebral fissure is not so frequent in the Rajbanshis in comparison to that in the Garo, Rabha and Kachari. The percentage occurrence of Mongolian eye fold shows a distinct trend of decrease from the Garo to the Rajbanshi through the Rabha and Kachari.

Oblique slit		Narrow Palpebral fissure		Medium Palpebral fissure		Mongolian fold	
Rh	92	Rh	70	Rj	39	G	56
G	82	G	65	G	33	Rh	48
K	72	K	53	Rh	28	K	35
Rj	39	Rj	21	K	27	Rj	11

Nose : In the case of nasal bridge and nasal septum the variation among the populations is not much. Though medium nasal depression occurs almost in equal frequencies in all the populations, the percentage of deep nasal depression is remarkably high in the Garo in comparison to that in the Rabhas, Kacharis and Rajbanshis.

Deep nasal depression		Medium nasal depression		Straight nasal bridge		Horizontal nasal septum	
G	44	Rh	49	Rh	58	K	71
Rj	13	G	47	G	56	G	66
Rh	12	Rj	47	K	56	Rh	59
K	7	K	41	Rj	52	Rj	59

Face : Persons with prognathism are met with more frequently in the Rabhas. From them the number of such persons gradually decreases to the Garo, then to the Kachari and finally to the Rajbanshis. Prominence of zygomatic arch shows considerable decrease from the Garos to the Rajbanshis through the Rabhas and Kacharis.

Prognathism		Marked zygomatic arch	
Rh	83	G	84
G	78	Rh	65
K	67	K	47
Rj	41	Rj	20

Lips: The percentage of lip of medium size decreases from the Garos to the Rajbanshis through Kacharis and Rabhas. The Rajbanshis have more number of thin lips than the others.

Lip of medium size	
G	97
K	84
Rh	83
Rj	77

Earlobe: The percentage of attached earlobe decreases from the Garo stage to the Rajbanshi-Rabha through Kachari. Consequently, free lobes are more frequent among the last three populations than the Garos.

Attached earlobe	
G	35
K	34
Rj	26
Rh	24

Body and Limbs: More number of sturdy persons are met with in the Garos. Their number decreases considerably to the Rajbanshi through the Kachari and Rabha.

Sturdy body and Limbs	
G	63
K	38
Rh	27
Rj	11

It will be evident from the above description that of all the populations the Rajbanshis show the highest number of terminations ending into decrease, while the Garos show the reverse trend, that is the highest number of termination ending into increase. Thus, the Rajbanshis may perhaps be considered as an end-product from the Garo base so far as the somatoscopic characters are concerned. This is in harmony with the result obtained from the anthropometric data, discussed hereafter.

The other two populations, namely, the Rabha and Kachari, occupy intermediate position in between the Garos on one hand and the Rajbanshis on the other.

A tendency towards finer or less marked physical features from the Rajbanshi stage is apparent in some characters. For instance, zygomatic arch which is marked among the Garos has become weakly marked among the Rajbanshis. Similarly, the high amount of prognathism is no longer present among the Rajbanshis. The eye slit has become straight, the palpebral fissure wide and the mongoloid fold less marked. The lips show a tendency towards thiner size. The growth of bread and moustache appears to have also increased. At the same time, a remarkable deterioration of body constitution appears to have occurred from the Garo to the Rajbanshi stage. The Garos are a sturdy people. This sturdiness is maintained to some extent by the Kacharis and Rabhas, while among the Rajbanshis sturdy persons are observed in a very low frequency. They are on the average of slender built.

Anthropometric Characters

A comparison of the anthropometric characters of the four populations under consideration may now be made in order to find out whether there are differences between the populations or not.

All together 13 measurements were taken and 6 indices were calculated. The measurements are: Stature, sitting height, head length, head breadth, head height, horizontal circumference of head, minimum frontal diameter, maximum bizygomatic breadth, bigonial breadth, nasal height, nasal breadth, upper facial height, and total facial height. The indices are: cephalic index, length-height index, breadth-height index, nasal index, upper facial index and total facial index.

The mean values have been compared by applying *t* test of significance to find out inter-population differences and similarities. The value of $t = 2.576$ and above has been taken as the standard of significance, because when the *t* value is between 2.576 and 3.460, p lies between .01 and .001, the degree of freedom being infinity.

It was found that the Garos differ from the Kacharis, Rabhas and Rajbanshis in 11 (57.89%), 5 (26.31%) and 13 (68.42%) characters respectively out of 19 characters (including indices). The Kacharis differ from the Rabhas in 10 (52.63%) and from the Rajbanshis in 12 (63.15%) characters. In 15 (78.94%) the Rabhas are different from the Rajbanshis (Table 2.1).

TABLE 2.1: **Inter-population differences in anthropometric characters**

		Measurements		Indices		Total	
		No.	%	No.	%	No.	%
Garo	–Kachari	7	53.84	4	66.66	11	57.89
	–Rabha	4	30.77	1	16.66	5	26.31
	—Rajbanshi	8	61.54	5	83.33	13	68.42
Kachari	–Rabha	7	53.84	3	50.00	10	52.63
	—Rajbanshi	8	61.54	4	66 66	12	63.15
Rabha	–Rajbanshi	10	76.92	5	83.33	15	78.94

As certain measurements are already included in the indices let us examine the measurements separately to avoid duplication in consideration of the characters. The table reveals greatest difference between the Rabhas and Rajbanshis and the least between the Rabhas and Garos. In all the cases differences are in more than 50% of the measurements, except between the Rabhas and Garos. In other words, the populations show variation in most of the characters suggesting that the populations are deviating from each other showing a tendency towards forming separate biological units. We have already mentioned about the prevailing legends of bifurcation af the Rabhas and Garos from a common branch. Anthropometric characters indicate that the Rabhas and Garos are more close to one another than the other populations.

Now, let us examine the trend of variation on the basis of means taking the Garos as the base line. The values have been put in the following order—the lowest value at the top and the highest at the bottom. The populations put within bracket show significant difference in respect of the character between the two populations.

Stature and Sitting height: The Garos appear to be the shortest of all. From the Garos the stature increases to the Rajbanshis through the Rabhas and Kacharis. The Garos differ significantly from the Kacharis and Rajbanshis, who again differ from the Rabhas also. Thus, in case of stature the position of the Garos and that of the Rajbanshis are in extreme. The mean of sitting height increases from the Garo to the Rajbanshi, than to the Rabha and finally to the Kachari. The Kacharis differ significantly from the Garos and Rajbanshis.

Stature		Sitting height	
G	159.49	G	83.21
Rh	161.25	Rj	83.95
K	163.05	Rh	84.36
Rj	163.63	K	84.49
(G-K; G-Rj; Rh-Rj)		(G-K; K-Rj)	

Head: We have taken into account four measurements on head and have calculated three indices.

Head length		Head breadth		Head height		Head circumference	
Rj	18.46	Rj	14.01	G	12.01	Rj	53.21
K	18.69	G	14.10	K	12.05	Rh	53.66
G	18.79	Rh	14.20	Rh	12.11	K	54.08
Rh	18.85	K	14.33	Rj	12.55	G	54.74
(G-Rj; K-Rh; Rh-Rj)		(G-K; K-Rj; Rh-Rj)		(G-Rj; K-Rj; Rh-Rj)		(G-K; G-Rj; G-Rh; Rh-Rj; K-Rj)	

Cephalic index		Length height index		Breadth height index	
G	75.17	G	63.96	Rj	79.45
Rh	75.40	K	64.38	G	85.35
Rj	76.10	Rh	64.45	Rh	85.53
K	76.74	Rj	66.55	K	85.77
(G-K; Rh-K)		(G-Rj; K-Rj; Rh-Rj)		(G-Rj; K-Rj; Rh-Rj)	

The Rajbanshi head is the shortest and narrowest of all, but is the highest of all. The mean of head height decreases from the Rajbanshis to the Garos through the Rabhas and Kacharis. They differ significantly from the other three populations, which are similar to each other. Because of head height the Rajbanshis are significantly different from the Rabhas, Kachari, and Rajbanshis, which do not show any difference among them in respect of length height index and breadth height index. The length height index decreases from the Rajbanshis to the Garos through the Rabhas and Kacharis. The head circumference decreases from the Garos to the Rajbanshis through the other two populations. Thus, in respect of head height, head circumference, and length height index the Garos and Rajbanshi occupy position at the two opposite ends. But head length, head breadth, cephalic index and breadth height index do not show such trend, though the Rajbanshis stand at one extreme end in case of head length, head breadth and breadth height index, and the Garos in case of cephalic index. The head of the Kacharis is the broadest and that of the Rabhas is the longest of all.

Face : Under face, besides facial height and bizygomatic breadth and the relative indices, minimum frontal and bigonial breadth will also be discussed.

Upper facial height		Total facial height		Bizygomatic breadth		Bigonial breadth	
Rh	6.61	Rh	11.20	Rj	13.24	Rj	9.75
Rj	6.68	Rj	11.31	Rh	13.50	K	9.99
G	6.70	G	11.34	K	13.70	G	10.10
K	6.79	K	11.43	G	13.87	Rh	10.70
(K-Rh)		(K-Rh)		(All)		(All except G-K)	

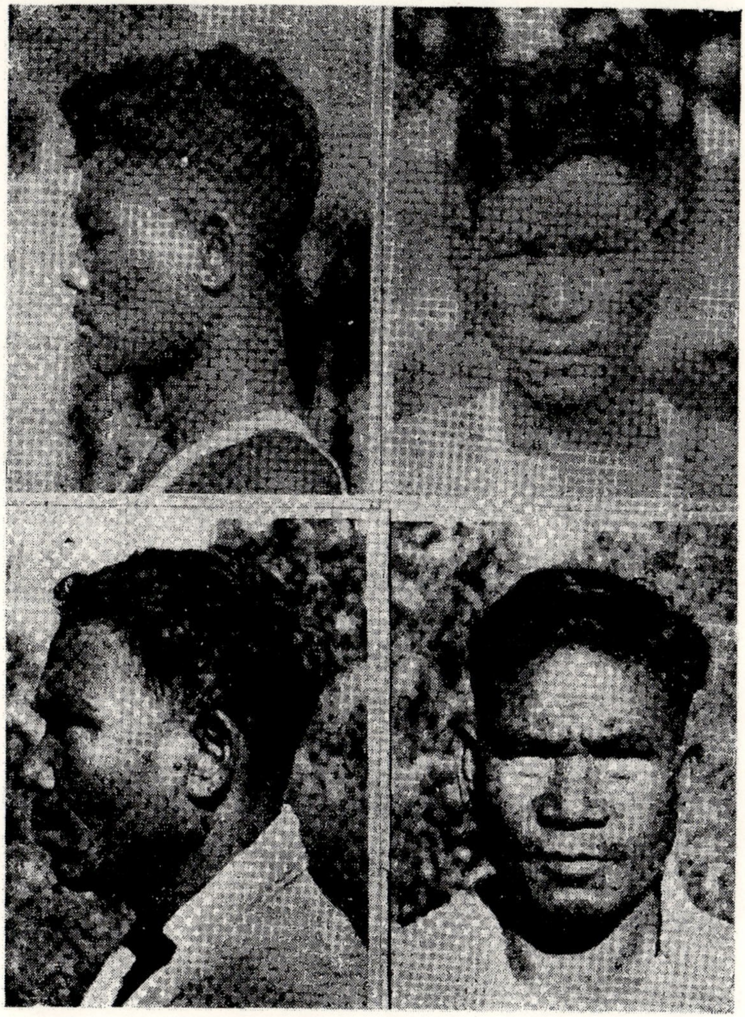

Plate 3 : RAEHA Males (Frontal and Profile views)

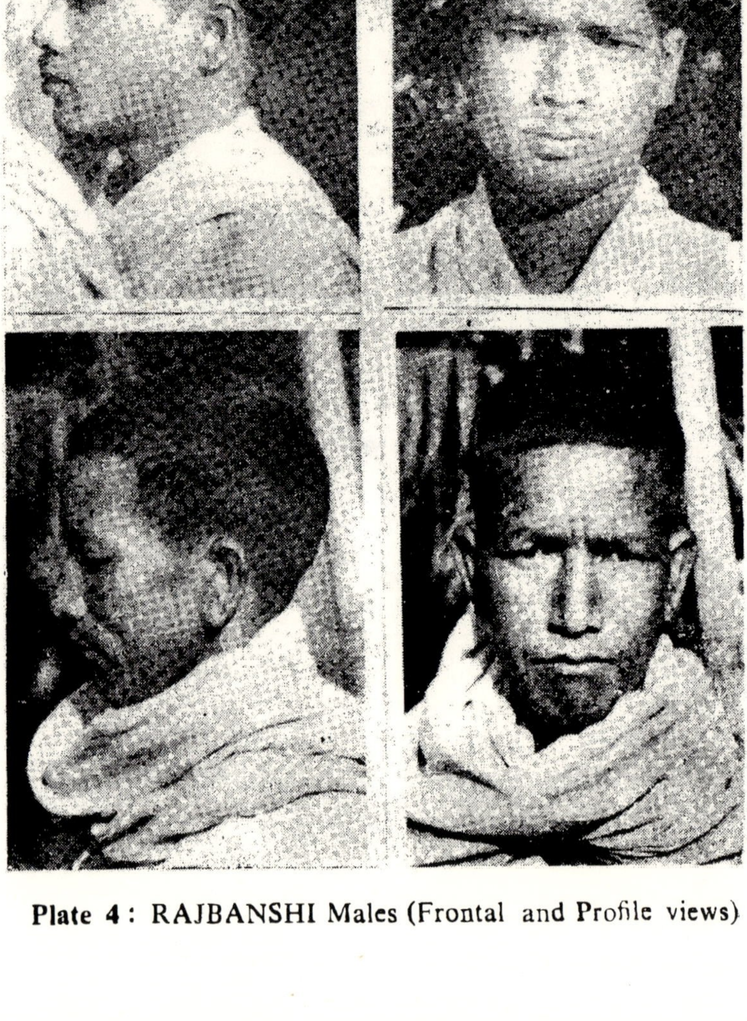

Plate 4 : RAJBANSHI Males (Frontal and Profile views)

Frontal diameter		Upper facial index		Total facial index	
Rh	10.22	G	48.23	K	80.25
Rj	10.48	Rh	48.73	G	82.10
K	10.50	K	49.64	Rh	83.04
G	10.62	Rj	50.33	Rj	85.65
(Rh-K; Rh-Rj)		(G-K; G-Rj, Rh-Rj)		(All except G-RH)	

In facial height, both upper and total, the populations do not exhibit much variation, the Rabhas and Kacharis being significantly different from one another. But in respect of bizygomatic breadth the four populations differ significantly from each other. Its mean gradually decreases from the Garos to the Kacharis, then to the Rabhas and finally to the Rajbanshis. As a result, upper facial index show a decrease from the Rajbanshis to the Garos through the Rabha-Kachari stage. As regards total facial index, the trend is though not exactly the same, yet is similar in the sense that the Rajbanshis showing the highest mean occupy an extreme, the other extreme being occupied by the Kacharis, followed by the Garos.

In respect of bigonial breadth the four populations show significant variation from each other. In contrast to the jaw, forehead region, i.e., minimum frontal diameter does not show much variation. Only the Rabhas are different from the Kacharis as well as Rajbanshis. In this measurement the Garos occupy one extreme position showing the highest value and the other extreme by the Rabhas followed by the Rajbanshis.

Nose : The nose show great variability among the four populations. The nasal index decreases from the Garo base line to the Rajbanshi through the Rabha-Kachari stage. So does nasal breadth. The trend is almost similar in nasal height also. Thus, in these three aspects the position of the Garos, showing broadest and shortest nose and highest nasal index, is at one extreme, while in respect of breadth and index the position of the Rajbanshis is at the opposite extreme.

Nasal height		Nasal breadth		Nasal index	
G	4.69	Rj	3.58	Rj	72.39
Rh	4.76	Rh	3.83	K	76.99
Rj	4.97	K	3.84	Rh	81.52
K	5.00	G	4.00	G	85.33
(All except G-Rh; K-Rj)		(All except K-Rh)		(All)	

It is apparent from the above description that in respect of (i) stature, (ii) head height, (iii) length height index, and (iv) upper facial index, there is only an increase in the mean values from the Garo base line to the end-product Rajbanshi. On the other hand, only a decrease in the mean values from the Garos to the Rajbanshis is seen with regard to (i) head circumference, (ii) bizygomatic breadth, (iii) nasal breadth and (iv) nasal index. In these 8 characters the Rabha-Rajbanshi stage is in intermediate position in between the Garo base line and the Rajbanshi end-product. In other characters both increase and decrease either from the Garos or from the Rajbanshis are observed. But in 12 characters, namely, (i) stature, (ii) sitting height, (iii) head height, (iv) head circumference, (v) Cephalic index, (vi) length height index, (vii) frontal diameter, (viii) bizygomatic breadth, (ix) nasal height, (x) nasal breadth, (xi) nasal index and (xii) upper facial index, the Garos are occupying a place at one extreme. Again in 13 characters the Rajbanshis are at one extreme. These characters are : (i) stature, (ii) head length, (iii) head breadth, (iv) head height, (v) head circumference, (vi) length height index, (vii) breadth height index, (viii) bizygomatic breadth, (ix) bigonial breadth, (x) nasal breadth, (xi) nasal index, (xii) upper facial index and (xiii) total facial index.

Thus, we can perhaps say that in general from the Garo base line to the Rajbanshi end-product, the stature has increased; the head has become shorter and broader; the face has become relatively longer and narrower; and the nose has become longer and narrower.

Dermatoglyphic traits

Of the dermatoglyphic traits the three types of finger pattern, namely, whorl, loop and arch, were examined. Hence only the percentile occurrence of the three types of pattern in the four populations has been taken into consideration. The data have been included in Table 2.2.

TABLE 2.2: **Percentile occurrence of the finger patterns in the four populations**

Population	No.	Whorl	Loops			Arches
			Radial	Ulnar	Total	
Garo	170	49.36	1.16	47.06	48.22	2.36
Rabha	295	50.66	1.55	46.24	47.79	1.55
Kachari	109	54.66	0.55	42.86	43.41	1.84
Rajbanshi	130	43.11	2.02	51.12	53.14	3.37

It appears that among the Garos and Rabhas whorls and loops occur in the ratio of almost 50 : 50. Among the Kacharis whorls (54.66%) are more frequent than loops (43.41%), while the reverse is true among the Rajbanshis (Whorls—43.11% and loops—54.13%). The Rajbanshis show more number of arches than the other three populations.

From the chi-square values, it is apparent that there is no significant difference between the Garos and Rabhas in respect of percentile occurrence of the three types of finger patterns. The Kachari-Garo value is significant at 2% level and the Kachari-Rabha value at 5% level. But the Rajbanshis differ significantly from each of the Garos, Rabhas and Kacharis.

Genetic Traits

The genetic traits considered in the present study are : ABO blood groups and Rh-factor.

ABO blood groups : Among the Garos and Rabhas A and B occur almost in equal frequencies, while among the Kacharis and Rajbanshis B is more frequent than A. Again, O occurs almost in equal frequencies in the Garos, Rabhas and Kacharis but its percentage is considerably higher in the Rajbanshis than in the first three (Table 2.3). Though the four populations do not show significant variation among them in respect of percentile occurrence of ABO blood groups, the Rajbanshi-Garo and the Rajbanshi-Rabha values are significant at 5% level.

TABLE 2.3 : **ABO Blood groups in the populations**

Population	No.	Percentile frequencies				Gene frequencies		
		O	A	A	AB	P	q	r
Garo	144	25.69	29.86	32.64	11.81	.2364	.2557	.5078
Rabha	126	24.60	30.95	31.75	12.70	.2493	.2547	.4960
Kachari	132	26.52	23.48	40.91	9.09	.1800	.2948	.5252
Rajbanshi	166	37.35	17.47	33.73	11.45	.1547	.2560	.5891

Rh-factor : It is a known fact that Rh-negative genes are very rare among the Mongoloids. Out of 555 persons examined only 6 are Rh-negative. All the Garos and the Kacharis are Rh-positive. Only one (0.79%) Rabha is Rh-negative. But out of 154 Rajbanshi individuals 5 (3.25%) are Rh-positive (Table 2.4). It has already been mentioned that the Rajbanshi is regarded as a Hindu caste and as such they are closer to the other Hindu castes. Therefore, perhaps they have received this gene from the other castes.

TABLE 2.4 : **Rh-factor in the Four Populations (in %)**

Population	No.	Rh +	Rh −
Garo	144	100.00	—
Rabha	126	99.21	0.79
Kachari	131	100.00	—
Rajbanshi	154	96.75	3.25

Our purpose to examine the physical feature was to see the trend of variation among these four populations, namely, the Garo, Rabha, Kachari and Rajbanshi, from the point of view of microevolution. In case of shape revealed by the percentile frequencies of different forms and types of somatoscopic characters and also in respect of size determined by anthropometric measurements, which are traits of continuous variation, these four populations may be arranged in order of microevolutionary sequence. The results clearly indicate that in this process the Garos may be regarded as the base line, while the Rajbanshi as the end-product. The Rabha-Kachari stage is intermediate between these two. We have already shown the modes of differentiation in physique.

The four populations form four distinct biological units each having its own distinctive characteristics. This differentiation in physique is further supported by dermatoglyphic trait like finger patterns. The Rajbanshis have assumed new characteristics in percentile occurrence of finger patterns. They are significantly different from each of the Rabhas, Garos and Kacharis. The Kacharis are also deviating from the Garos and Rabhas. The similarities between the Garos and Rabhas with regard to finger pattern is in conformity with the results obtained by analysing the scopic and metric traits.

In respect of ABO blood groups also though not the same, yet a similar picture is observed. The Rajbanshis differ from the Garos and Rabhas at 5 per cent level of significance, the last two being more similar to one another than any two other populations. This suggests that variability is more in respect of metric traits than in genetic traits like ABO blood groups. Ploymorphism in scopic and metric traits are produced by involvement of more number of genes, hence chance of plasticity is greater in such traits.

We do not venture to suggest any definite explanation of these small variation. A large number of factors may be involved in this process. We must not forget about the ecotypes. In the present study the environment varies in three manners : firstly, the hilly habitat of the Garos; secondly the partially similar habitat of some of the Rabhas; and thirdly, the river valley of the others. How far and what way these three variable environments influence different types of physical features are not perfectly known. The behaviour of the different physical measurements in different environments need study to arrive at in definite conclusions. We referred to the process of detribalization. The four populations are in three stages of detribalization. This aspect also needs proper investigation. However, it is not meant in any way that detribalization has brought about these changes in physical features. The way of life including numerous variables like house type, food habit, drinking habit, economic pursuit, marriage pattern, is not the same for all the four populations. Each variable is playing its own role in influencing the biological aspect of the people. Again, hybridization is another very potent factor in causing physical changes. Thus, a host of factors appear to be related with each physical trait in particular and the whole process of variation in general. In such type of study, it is very difficult to isolate one factor from the other as they are interrelated. Therefore, we must admit that we have made an attempt to show the range and trend of variation among these four populations, which may be called microevolutionary in nature, without pretending to offer any explanation for such variation.

Microevolutionary Trend in the Khasis*

3

The Khasi and Jaintia hills, the eastern part of the state of Meghalaya, is the homeland of a tribe called the Khasi, a member of the Indo-Mongoloid group (Map No. 1). They speak a dialect of the Mon-Khmer linguistic group and in that sense they are an Austro-Asiatic people. The Khasis are a matriarchal people. In a family authority is vested on the mother. Descent is matrilineal. Succession is through the female line. The daughters inherit the property. After marriage they do not go to live in the house of the husband.

The Khasi tribe is divided into four main divisions : the Khynriam; the Pnar or Jaintia, who are also called synteng; the Bhoi and the War. The Khynriams live in the western part of the Khasi country, while the Pnars occupy the Jaintia hills lying on the eastern side. The Bhois are met with in the low hills towards north and northwest of the region. The Wars inhabit the slopes and deep valleys towards south. The southern region where the Wars live is a narrow strip of land with high and stiff slopes abruptly terminating at the Surama valley. On the other hand, the northern region, the habitat of the Bhois, forms an extensive plateau with flat lands and open valleys; gradually sloping towards the Brahmaputra valley. The altitude of the Bhoi country ranges up to about 800 metre. Between the southern and northern regions lies the central part, which is an irregular plateau at a much higher elevation, the highest peak at the heart of the Khynriam country being about 1950 metre high. Small ranges of hills with extensive

* The present study is based on the author's book entitled *Variation in Physical Characteristics in the Khasi Population of North East India* published in 1978.

valleys amidst then forms the central plateau of the Jaintia hills, where the Pnars live.

There is no bar against intermarriage among the four divisions. But in practice, intermarriage is not frequent, specially in the interior regions, where people of only one subdivision live. This is because of mainly two reasons—firstly, isolation caused by geographical condition of the country and secondly, certain socio-cultural factors associated with marriage and other aspects of the way of life. In such areas, where people of two subdivisions live in close proximity, intermarriage takes place. But the present data were collected from the interiors where intermarriage is very rare. Hence, we have at our hand four distinct samples from four divisions inhabiting four different regions of the Khasi and Jaintia hills.

The Khasis have drawn attention of anthropologists as well as linguistics because of several reasons. The linguistics are interested for the reason that the Khasis speaking Mon-Khmer language form an isolated pocket amidst populations all belonging to Tibeto-Burman linguistic family. Many physical anthropologists have described their physical characters considering the Khasi population as a while and also of the Pnars. We shall consider the four divisions separately to examine the nature and trend of variation. For this purpose we shall examine characters of three categories : anthropometric measurements; genetic traits like ABO blood groups and taste sensitivity to PTC; and dermatoglyphic traits like finger patterns.

Anthropometric characters

Thirteen measurements, namely, stature, sitting height, head length, head breadth, head height, horizontal circumference of head, minimum frontal diameter, maximum bizygomatic breadth, bigonial breadth, upper facial height, total facial height, nasal height and nasal breadth, were taken on 100 adult male individuals of each of the four divisions of the Khasi. From the measurements six indices like cephalic, length-height, breadth-height, upper facial, total facial and nasal, were calculated.

First, it was attempted to find out if the four divisions may really be considered as forming parts of a single unit

Khasi, or if significant differences do exist among the means of the four divisions. For that purpose *F*-test $(F = \frac{\text{mean square between groups}}{\text{mean square within group}})$ was applied. The results of *F*-test reveal that most of the values are high suggesting significant differences among the four divisions. Thus, the Khasi tribe as a whole apparently is not homogeneous. Only in gross physique, characterized by stature and sitting height, the four divisions may be looked upon as belonging to one biological unit. Hence, it is justified to consider each of the divisions separately to examine the trend of variation.

Now let us have a general anthropometric picture of each of the divisions of the Khasi tribe. The Khynriams are short in stature. They are mesocephalic, hypsicephalic and acrocephalic in the majority. The face is euryprosopic and is of euryne type. They have platyrrhine nose, but the frequencies of mesorrhine is also high.

The Pnars are characterised by very short stature. They are dolichocephalic and hypsicephalic. Though they have metriocephalic means, the frequencies of the other two types, tapeinocephaly and acrocephaly, are also considerably high. The face is of mesene type. In them mesoprosopy predominates. The nose is mesorrhine.

The Bhois have short stature. They are characterised by mesocephalic, hypsicephalic and acrocephalic head. The face is of mesene and mesoprosopic type. The nose is mesorrhine.

The Wars are short in stature. The head is mesocephalic, hypsicephalic and acrocephalic. The face is euryprosopic and of euryene type. Though the mean nasal index is mesorrhine, there is a tendency towards platyrrhiny.

The mean values of anthropometric characters have been included in Table 3.1.

The head of the Pnars is dolichocephalic, while the others have mesocephalic heads; and thus the Pnars differ from the remaining three divisions. The head of the Pnar is the longest, while that of the Bhoi the shortest. In between these two extremes, similar to one another, lie the Khynriam and the War. In head breadth we find as in head length, an increase from the Bhoi over the War to the Khynriam. The Pnars, however, with maximum head length show only a medium

TABLE 3.1: **Mean Values of Anthropometric Characters**

Measurements (in mm)	Khynriam (N=100) Mean ±S.E.	Pnar (N=100) Mean ±S.E	Bhoi (N=100) Mean± S.E	War (N=100) Mean ±S.E
St.	1566.2±5.2	1573.5±5.9	1570.0±5.7	1556.8±5.5
S.H.	823.6±3.4	811.2±3.8	823.6±3.3	815.7±3.3
H.L.	188.2±0.5	191.0±0.6	183.4±0.5	186.7±0.6
H.B.	146.4±0.6	145.3±0.4	142.4±0.5	144.3±0.5
H.H.	122.9±0.9	119.2±0.9	127.7±0.8	119.0±1.1
H.C.H.	546.0±0.2	545.9±1.3	517.9±1.6	541.6±1.3
M.F.D.	104.1±0.5	100.5±0.5	104.6±0.5	105.1±0.6
M.B.B.	135.1±0.4	135.1±0.5	134.5±0.5	134.7±0.4
B.B.	101.6±0.5	102.2±0.5	99.5±0.5	100.5±0.5
U.F.H.	63.6±0.5	65.6±0.5	66.4±0.5	63.4±0.5
T.F.H.	110.7±0.6	114.0±0.6	113.3±0.6	110.5±0.6
N.H.	45.4±0.1	47.9±0.3	48.7±0.4	45 8±0.4
N.B.	39.2±0.3	37.2±0 2	39.5±0 3	38.0±0.3
Indices				
C.I.	77.73±0.34	75.83±0.28	77.67±0.28	77.38±0.35
L.H.I.	65.21±0.50	62.64±0.46	69.46±0.48	67.47±0.62
B.H.I.	83.93±0.67	82.39±0.61	89.54±0.62	82.46±0.81
U.F.I.	46.12±0.36	48.66±0.37	49.41±0.39	47.39±0.42
T.F.I.	82.00±0.44	84.58±0.46	84.32±0.50	82.01±0.46
N.I.	86.63±0.95	78.00±0 71	81.57±0.91	82.61±0.99

breadth. These findings are in accordance with the horizontal circumference of head. The head of the Bhoi is the smallest, while the Khynriam and Pnar with about the same circumference show the largest heads.

The Bhois have the highest head and thus in this regard they are significantly different from the other three divisions. Each of the divisions has hypsicephalic heads. The Bhois have the highest mean and the Pnars the lowest. The same is true in respect of breadth-height index also. But the Pnars, the

Bhois and the Wars have acrocephalic heads, while the Khynriams have metrocephalic heads.

The four divisions do not show significant differences among them as regards the breadth of the face as revealed by the values of bizygomatic breadth. But in the height of the face, differences are observed. So far as the upper part of the face is concerned, the Bhoi value is the highest. They have the narrowest face shape. A very similar index has been calculated for the Pnar. Both these divisions possess also an almost equally high total facial index. The upper as well as the total face look somewhat broader and lower in the Khynriam and the War.

The Khynriams have the broadest nose and the Pnars the narrowest, as revealed by the values of nasal index. The Khynriam nose is platyrrhine, whereas the other three divisions have mesorrhine noses. They are very closely followed by the Khynriams. The Bhois have the highest nose also, and the Khynriams the lowest. They are closely followed by the Wars.

The inter-division differences and similarities have been found out by applying t-test of significance. It appears that there is no significant difference between the Khynriams and Wars. The other divisions show significant differences among them in respect of many characteristics. Only with regard to stature, sitting height and bizygomatic breadth a common similarity among the four divisions is observed.

The Bhois differ from the Khynriams in having shorter, narrower, smaller, but higher heads, higher faces and higher noses. They have shorter, narrower, smaller and higher heads than the Pnars also. But the nose is broader. The Bhois have shorter, smaller but higher heads, higher faces and higher noses than the Wars.

The Pnars have longer heads, higher faces and higher and narrower noses than the Khynriam. They differ from the latter in those indices also where the length of the head is involved. The Pnars differ from the Wars in the same way as they do with regard to the Khynriam, i.e., they have longer heads, higher faces and higher and narrower noses. The Pnars have longer, broader and lower heads, and narrower noses than the Wars. The face is similar in both the divisions. The Pnars have longer, broader and lower heads and narrower noses than the Bhois.

The Khynriams show a very close resemblance to the Wars. They have longer, broader, larger but lower heads, lower faces and lower noses than the Bhois, and shorter heads, lower faces, lower and broader noses than the Pnars.

The Wars have longer and lower heads, lower faces and lower noses than the Bhois. The Wars differ from the Pnars in having shorter heads, lower faces, lower and broader noses.

In general, it can be said that of all the four divisions, the Bhois have the shortest, narrowest, smallest, but highest heads. The upper part of the face is the highest in them, which is reflected in upper facial index also. On the other hand, the Pnars have the longest head, narrowest face and the narrowest nose. Among them the mean values of length-height and breadth-height indices are the lowest. Contrary to the Pnars, the Khynriams have the broadest head, broadest face and the broadest nose. This is, however, in shape. The Wars resemble the Khynriams.

The above analysis reveals that only the Khynriams and the Wars are very close to one another. The others deviate from each other.

It appears that the Bhois are in the process of separating from the other divisions and that they are heading towards forming separate entity.

Next to the Bhois stand the Pnars. In this connection, mention may be made that the Pnars are conscious of their separate identity, and therefore, recently on demand, they were able to put a administrative boundary between their territory and the territory of the other three. There are some culturul differences also between the two.

While describing the anthropometric characters, the four divisions were found to present differences. The *t*-test revealed a closer affinity between the Khynriam and the War, and a greater distance between the Bhoi and the Pnar. The results of the *F*-test also reveal significant differences among the four divisions in respect of most of the characters, thus confirming the results obtained from *t*-test.

Taste Sensitivity to PTC

In all 838 Khasi individuals (Table 3.2) were tested for taste sensitivity to phenylthiocarbamide. As the chi-square values do not signify sexual differences in any of the populations, the two sexes have been pooled for the purpose of comparison. The frequency of non-tasters is somewhat higher in the Bhois (21.09%) than that in each of the Pnars (17.06%), Wars (12.29%) and Khynriam (11.26%). In this respect the Bhois significantly differ from the Khynriams as well as the Wars. The Pnar-Bhoi value is not significant.

TABLE 3.2: **Tasters and non-tasters among the four divisions of the Khasi**

	No.	Taster %	Non-taster %	Gene frequency T	t
Khynriam					
Male	132	88.63	11.36	.663	.337
Female	90	88.11	11.11	.667	.333
Total	222	88.74	11.26	.665	.335
Pnar					
Male	80	81.25	18.75	.567	.433
Female	90	84.44	15.55	.606	.394
Total	170	82.94	17.06	.587	.413
Bhoi					
Male	120	77.50	22.50	.526	.474
Female	90	78.88	21.11	.541	.459
Total	210	78.09	21.90	.532	.468
War					
Male	141	86.52	13.48	.633	.367
Female	95	89.48	10.52	.676	.324
Total	236	87.71	12.29	.650	.350

As regards the mean values of taste threshold (Table 3.3) the Bhoi mean (9.09) is significantly higher than the Khynriam

(7.59) and War (7.76) means. The Pnar mean (8.80) is similar to the Bhoi mean.

Thus, in respect of this trait also the deviating tendency of the Bhoi is noteworthy.

TABLE 3.3: **Mean values of test threshold of tasters (Khasi)**

Divisions	Mean ± S.E.
Khynriam	7.59 ± .11
Pnar	8.80 ± .15
Bhoi	9.09 ± .13
War	7.76 ± .11

ABO Blood Groups

In all 821 individuals (Table 3.4) were tested for their ABO blood groups. Among all the four divisions A occurs more frequently than B. The frequency of B is higher in the Bhois in comparison to that in the other three divisions. The reverse is true with regard to frequency of O. In respect of occurrence of A the differences among the four divisions are comparatively smaller.

TABLE 3.4: **Percentile occurrence of ABO blood groups in the Khasi populations**

	Percentile frequencies					Gene frequencies		
	No.	O	A	B	AB	p	q	r
Khynriam	202	49.0	29.2	18.7	2.1	.1776	.1164	.7060
Pnar	197	52.8	33.5	11.6	2.1	.1984	.0711	.7305
Bhoi	192	38.7	30.4	23.0	7.8	.2184	.1694	.6161
War	230	55.7	28.6	11.9	3.7	.1785	.0822	.7393

The chi-square values indicate that the Bhois differ significantly from the Pnars as well as the Wars in respect of frequency distribution of the ABO blood groups. The other values are not statistically significant. Thus, the Bhois stand apart from the two of the other three divisions of the same tribe.

Dermatoglyphic traits

Finger prints of 587 Khasi individuals (Table 3.5) were examined. The three main finger patterns, namely, whorl, loop (radial and ulnar) and arch, have been identified for classification. As there was no significant sexual variation, the two sexes have been combined for the purpose of intra-tribal comparison.

TABLE 3.5: **Percentile occurrence of Finger Patterns**

(Male+Female)

Populations No.	M	F	Total	Whorls	Radial	Loops Ulnar	Total	Arches
Khynriam	67	97	164	37.38	2.93	56.89	59.82	2.80
Pnar	95	92	187	38.77	2.14	56.73	58.87	2.36
Bhoi	32	39	71	45.63	1.55	51.97	53.52	0.85
War	98	67	165	38.93	3.03	55.18	58.21	2.86

Each of the four divisions of the Khasi tribe possesses more loops than whorls. The Bois have comparatively more whorls, and fewer arches and loops than the other three divisions. Chi-square test reveals that these differences between the Bhoi on one hand and each of the Khynriams, Pnars and Wars, on the other hand, and statistically significant. The other groups do not differ significantly from each other.

Thus, it appears that with regard to percentile occurrence of finger patterns, the Bhois are different from each of the other three divisions of the Khasi tribe. But it is not so with regard to total ridge counts. The four divisions of the Khasi do not deviate significantly from each other in this respect (Table 3.6).

TABLE 3.6: **Total ridge counts**

Populations		Mean ±S.E.
Khynriam	(Male+Female)	128.30±6.11
Pnar	(Male+Female)	132.06±5.20
Bhoi	(Male+Female)	139.78±6.13
War	(Male+Female)	131.51±5.41

We have examined the nature and range of interdivision variability with regard to metric traits and have noted that only the Khynriams and Wars are very similar to one another; otherwise interdivision variability is quite significant suggesting that each of the divisions is heading towards acquiring a somewhat different physique. This sort of separating tendency is more remarkable in the Bhois and the Pnars than in the other two divisions, the Khynriams and Wars. On the other hand, we do not see the same picture with regard to the other traits, i.e. ABO blood groups, finger patterns and taste sensitivity to PTC. In respect of these traits a common agreement among the Khynriams, Pnars and Wars is apparent. Thus, interdivision variability is more with regard to anthropometric characters than genetic traits. Incidentally it may be pointed out that a similar phenomenon was observed in the Boro population also.

The Bhois, however, present an entirely different picture. They deviate in all the traits, namely, anthropometry, ABO blood groups, finger patterns and taste sensitivity to PTC, from each of the Khynriams, Pnars and Wars. They appear to have already formed a separate biological unit distinguishable from the other three divisions of the same parental group. Though the Pnars have not behaved exactly like the Bhois, in them also this sort of deviating tendency is quite clear.

We must admit that at present we are not in a position to offer definite explanation of such behaviour of the Bhois and Pnars. However, we may think of difference in altitudes. We have already stated that the Bhois live in lower altitude and towards north the altitude of the Khasi hills gradually lowers down to reach the Brahmaputra valley, where other tribal

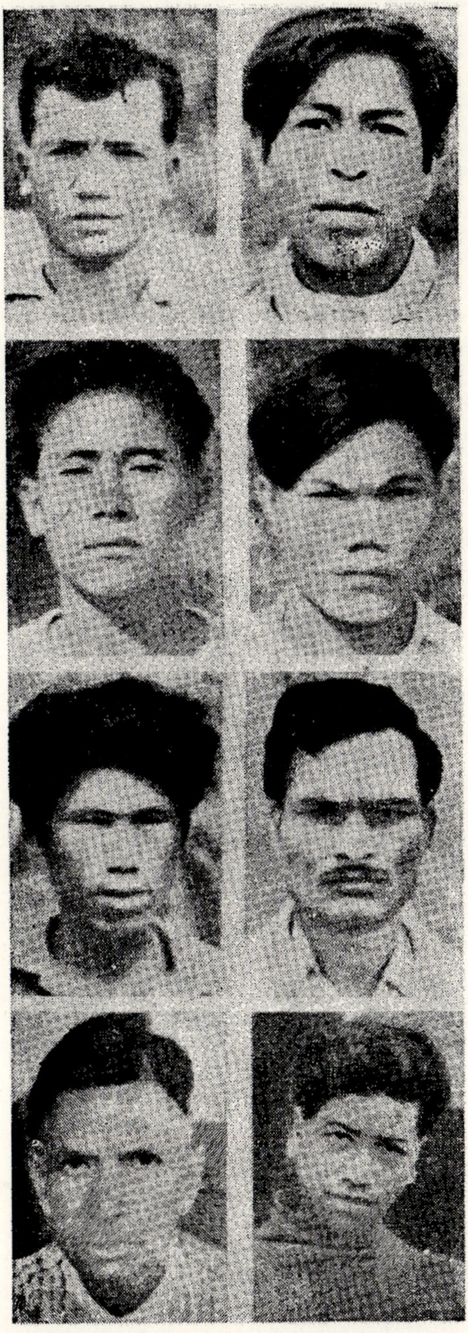

Plate 5 : Four Sections of the KHASI (Males)
(Frontal and Profile views)

populations are also met with. Therefore, the possibility of gene inflow to the Bhois from the neighbouring population cannot completely be ruled out. This is, however, an assumption only, because unfortunately at the present we do not have necessary data to test this hypothesis. As regards the Pnars we have already mentioned about their consciousness to preserve their own identity, which may have helped to keep them isolated, both socially and biologically, resulting in their separation from the other division of the same stock.

Perhaps we may conclude that whatever might be the causes, a comprehensive picture of the nature and range of variation in physical anthropological traits in the Khasi population gives a clear indication of a microevolutionary trend among them.

Microevolutionary Trend In the Chutiyas* 4

The Chutiyas form one of the very old populations of Assam. They are mostly confined to the Upper Assam districts of Dibrugarh, Sibsagar and Lakhimpur (Map No.1). They had their own kingdom in that region. When the Ahoms, a Tai population, came to Assam in the early part of the thirteenth century, the Chutiyas has to resist their aggression and fight continued for several centuries. Ultimately the Ahoms overrun the Chutiya country. Some of the Chutiyas got admixtured with the Ahoms and as a result, today we find a section of the Chutiyas, called the Ahom-Chutiya.

The Chutiyas are Indo-Mongoloid. Linguistically, they belong to the Assam-Burmese group of the Tibeto-Burman family. But long back they accepted Assamese language and now they form an integral part of the Assamese speaking Assamese.

The Chutiyas have been subdivided into some sections. The number of such sections varies from author to author. As has already been mentioned one section is known as the Ahom-Chutiya, which suggests admixture between Ahom and Chutiya in that section. Unfortunately, we do not have any data on physical anthropology of this section to examine the extent of admixture between these two populations. Our data are from two other sections of the Chutiyas—one, the Deuri-Chutiya and the other, the Hindu-Chutiya. The Deuri-Chutiya (hereinafter called Deuri) sample was drawn from Dibrugarh district and

* The data have been taken from two 'Study Reports' prepared under a Research Project sponsored by the U.G.C. The study reports are : (1) A comparative study of physical anthropology of five Mongoloid populations of Assam and (2) Biosocial profile of five Mongoloid populations of Assam, by B.M. Das, Priya Bala Das avd Renuka Das.

the Hindu-Chutiya (hereinafter called Chutiya) from Sibsagar and Dibrugarh districts. These two are adjacent districts in the south bank of the river Brahmaputra.

The Deuris form the priestly section of the Chutiya. They seem to have preserved the traditional socio-cultural identity of the Chutiyas. As the name implies the Chutiyas (Hindu-Chutiya) are Hindu. Socio-culturally they are very much like the other Assamese Hindu castes. They marry among themselves like other Hindu castes. However, the Deuris are also Hinduised.

Among the Deuris the percentage of joint family (64%) is very high in comparison to that of nuclear family (36%). The reverse is true in the case of the Chutiyas where joint and nuclear families are found in 30 per cent and 70 per cent respectively. Among the Chutiyas, the families are of medium (number of persons 4 to 6) to big (number of persons 7 to 9) size, their percentages being 39 per cent and 51 per cent respectively, while among the Deuris very big (number of persons 10+) and big families are often found, the percentages being 54 per cent and 38 per cent respectively.

The Deuris show a sex-ratio of 51 (M): 49(F), while the Chutiyas 53 (M) : 47(F). Girls of both the populations marry at the age between 15 and 20 years, the mean being $18.40 \pm .27$ years and $18.01 \pm .18$ years in the Deuris and Chutiyas respectively. The mean age at menarch of the Deuri girls ($13.37 \pm .11$ years) is significantly higher than that of the Chutiya girls ($12.50 \pm .11$ years). However, the first baby is born almost at the same age, the means being $19.83 \pm .28$ years and $19.39 \pm .19$ years in the Deuris and Chutiyas respectively.

The mean conception is 5.62 in the Deuris as against 4.58 in the Chutiyas. Pregnancy wastage is slightly higher in the Chutiyas (1.37%) than that in the Deuris (0.77%). After child-mortality the percentage of still-alive children is 94.2 in the Deuris and 92.2 in the Chutiyas.

Now we propose to examine the data on physical anthropology on these two populations; namely, Deuri and Chutiya. We will take into consideration certain anthropometric genetic, dermatoglyphic and behavioural traits in the present study.

Anthropometric characters

The following measurements were taken on adult male members of these two populations : stature, head length, head breadth, head height, head circumference, bizygomatic breadth. upper facial height, total facial height, nasal height and nasal breadth. Six indices, namely, cephalic, length height, breadth height, upper facial, total facial and nasal, were calculated. The mean values of these measurements and indices have been given in Table 4.1.

TABLE 4.1: **Anthropometric Characters: Values of *t***

Measurements (in cm)	Deuri (N=99) Mean ± S.E.	Chutiya (N=83) Mean ± S.E.	Values of *t* Deuri – Chutiya
St.	163.86 ± .48	164.11 ± .55	0.34
S.H.	83.95 ± .32	84.13 ± .36	0.38
H.L.	18.38 ± .05	18.38 ± .07	0
H.B.	14.63 ± .05	14.68 ± .07	0.56
H.H.	13.69 ± .15	13.63 ± .18	0.32
H.C.H.	55.71 ± .16	55.16 ± .21	2.12
M.B.B.	13.54 ± .05	13.44 ± .06	1.25
N.H.	5.21 ± .05	5.04 ± .05	2.42
N.B.	3.80 ± .03	3.78 ± .03	0.15
U.F.H.	7.00 ± .06	6.76 ± .06	3.00
T.F.H.	11.44 ± .06	11.59 ± .08	1.50
Indices			
C.I	79.31 ± .35	80.36 ± .41	1.94
L.H.I.	74.37 ± .80	74.05 ± .90	0.27
B.H.I.	93.71 ± .95	92.66 ± 1.24	0.72
N.I.	73.63 ± .86	75.59 ± .90	1.58
U.F.I.	51.65 ± .46	50.24 ± .48	2.14
T.F.I.	85.28 ± .46	85.83 ± .60	0.72

In size, as obtained by the measurements and in shape, as revealed by the indices, there are no significant differences between the Chutiyas and Deuris. One is indistinguishable from the other on the basis of mean values of the characters concerned.

Genetic traits

Two genetic traits were examined—one ABO blood groups and the other taste sensitivity to PTC. In respect of the percentile occurrence of ABO blood groups the Chutiyas are significantly different from the Deuris (Table 4.2). Among the Chutiyas (47.28%) O occurs in a much higher percentage than in the Deuris (28.50%). Though in both the populations A is more frequent than B, the percentage of A gene is much higher in the Deuri (30.88%) than in the Chutiya (19.93%).

TABLE 4.2: **ABO Blood Groups**

Populations	No.	Percentile frequencies				Gene frequencies		
		O	A	B	AB	P	q	r
Deuri	200	28.50	44.00	19.50	8.00	.3088	.1494	.5418
Chutiya	184	47.28	31.52	16.85	4.35	.1993	.1123	.6884

Chi-squre value 15.36 P lies between .01—.001 d.f. 3

Though members of both the sexes were tested for taste sensitivity to PTC, the samples of the two sexes were pooled together as there was no significant sexual difference (Table 4.3). The percentage of non-taster is 27.36 in the Deuri and 30.00 in the Chutiya. Therefore, there is no significant difference between these two populations. Again, the mean of taster threshold is 5.87±.18 in the Deuri and 5.98±.18 in the Chutiya. Hence in respect of mean also the two populations are similar to one another.

Dermatoglyphic traits

The two populations have been compared in respect of percent-

TABLE 4.3 : **Taste Sensitivity to PTC**

Population	Sex	No.	Non-Taster	Taster	Gene frequencies	
			%	Mean ± S.E.	T	t
Deuri	M	100	32.00	5.63 ± .18	.4343	.5657
	F	101	22.77	6.11 ± .18	.5228	.4772
	T	201	27.36	5.87 ± .18	.4769	.5231
Chutiya	M	104	29.81	5.83 ± .28	.4540	.5460
	F	86	30.23	6.72 ± .31	.4502	.5498
	T	190	30.00	5.98 ± .29	.4523	.5477

Population		Chi-square values	P lies between
Deuri	M×F	2.155	.20 — .10
Chutiya	M×F	0.004	.95 — .90
Deuri×Chutiya		0.333	.70 — .50
	d.f. 1		

ile occurrence of finger patterns (Table 4.4) and three main line formulae (Table 4.5).

In respect of finger patterns, sexual variation is significant among the Chutiyas, though not among the Deuris. Therefore, the two sexes are compared separately. The Deuri males do not differ significantly from the Chutiya males, but the females do. In the Deuri females whorl is more frequent than loop, while the reverse is true in the Chutiya female. Again, in the Deuri females arch is much more frequent than in the Chutiya females.

As regards main line formulae there is no significant sexual variation in both the populations. Hence sex was ignored while making comparison between the two. Among the Deuris (31%) the formulae 7. 5. 5.—is much more frequent than among the Chutiyas (20%). On the other hand, the type 11. 9. 7.—is much more frequent in the Chutiya (30%) than in the Deuris (17%). As a result, in respect of this aspect of dermatoglyphics the Chutiyas differ from the Deuris.

Behavioural traits

Five behavioural traits, namely, hand clasping, arm folding, handedness, dominant eye and tongue rolling, form a part of the present study (Table 4.6). As there was no significant sexual variation the samples on the two sexes were pooled and then compared. In respect of arm folding and handedness there is no significant difference between the Chutiyas and Deuris. But with regard to hand clasping, dominant eye and tongue rolling the differences between the two populations are significant.

From the above comparative account of the two populations it is evident that unlike the Boro and Khasi populations there is no difference in anthropometric characters between the Chutiyas and Deuris. But in certain other categories of characters, like ABO blood groups, dermatoglyphics and some behavioural traits, differences are apparent. Therefore, though the Deuris and Chutiyas are two sections of the same population, perhaps it could be said that they show a tendency to deviate from one another in certain physical anthropological characters. The two are heading to form two biological units.

TABLE 4.4 : **Finger Pattern**

Population	Sex	No.	Whorl	Loop			Arch
				Ulnar	Radial	Total	
Deuri	M	57	54.56	40.70	2.81	43.51	1.93
	F	58	54.14	40.34	1.90	42.24	3.62
Sexual variation : Chi-square value 3.05 : P lies between .10 — .05 d.f. 2							
Chutiya	M	62	49.19	45.16	2.10	47.26	3.55
	F	58	41.55	55.69	2.07	57.76	0.69
Sexual variation : Chi-square value 21.47 : P lies between .001— d.f. 2							

	Chi-square value	P lies between
Male Deuri × Chutiya	5.38	.10 — .05
Female ,, × ,,	35.12	.001 —

d.f. 2

TABLE 4.5 : **Main Line Formulae**

Population	Sex	No.	11. 9. 7.— (a) %	9. 7. 7.— (b) %	7. 5. 5.— (c) %
Deuri	M	49	20.40	24.48	28.57
	F	50	16.00	32.00	34.00
Chutiya	M	51	24.50	33.32	24.50
	F	49	36.73	30.61	15.30

Population	Chi-square value	P lies between
Deuri Male × Deuri Female	1.50	.50 — .30
Chutiya Male × Chutiya Female	4.65	.10 — .05
Deuri × Chutiya	11.36	.01 — .001

d.f. 2

TABLE 4.6 : **Behavioural Traits**

	R-Type		Chi-square values	P lies between
	Deuri	Chutiya		
Hand clasping	92.04	62.31	48.82	.001 –
Arm Folding	21.89	25.79	0.82	.80 — .70
Handedness	98.01	100.00	3.81	.10 — .05
Dominant Eye	74.63	61.58	7.67	.01 – .001
		Positive type		
Tongue rolling	52.74	40.53	5.85	.02 — .01

d.f. 1

In this connection it should be mentioned that the ecotype of the two populations is the same. Both inhabit the fertile plains of the Brahmaputra river. Their habits and activities are also similar. Metric traits show more variability when geographical environments are different. These aspects of the Chutiyas and Deuris cannot be totally ignored. These factors may be responsible for not bringing about changes in the metric traits.

As regards differences in the other traits we can look for some other reasons. The Deuris and Chutiyas have no separate territory of their own. In the Brahmaputra valley they live along with other populations. Therefore, there are possibilities of flow of genes from the neighbouring populations, which form a numerically dominant group more particularly the Ahoms. We have already mentioned that there is a section called Ahom-Chutiya, indicating admixture with the Ahoms. Though we have not collected data from this section, the possibility of acquiring genes by the present sample of the Chutiyas cannot be completely ruled out. Unknown ancestors of some of the Chutiyas may be Ahom. But this possibility is less in the case of the Deuris. Because they are a priestly section and they are custodian of the Chutiya socio-cultural tradition. They form a closed society. This social separation of the Deuris along with gene flow from the Ahom to the Chutiyas may lead to biological differences between the two. If this hypothesis is true, we should get more similarities between the Ahoms and Chutiyas than between the Ahoms and Deuris.

An Ahom sample was also collected in the course of investigation. Like the Chutiyas the Ahoms also possess a high percentage of individuals of O blood groups. The ABO gene frequencies of the Ahoms and Chutiyas are similar. As a matter of fact, while the Deuris differ significantly from the Ahoms, the difference between the Chutiyas and Ahoms is not statistically significant. However, with regard to taste sensitivity to PTC no such differences and similarities are observed. But in finger patterns the Chutiyas are similar to the Ahoms, while the Deuris are not. Thus, perhaps the above explanations for differences and similarities between the Deuri and Chutiya are tenable.

Whatever might be the possible reasons, the fact remains that though the Chutiyas and Deuris have a common ancestral group, they are showing a tendency to separate from one another to form two biological units, suggesting microevolutionary trend.

Summary and Conclusion 5

Experiment can be carried on upon the experimental animals in the laboratory. But experiment can not be done upon man and anthropology is a subject which deals with man. Anthropology is basically a field science. The world itself is a laboratory for the anthropologists. The nature itself provides laboratory facilities to the researchers in anthropology. An anthropologist is to identify his laboratory where results are furnished by the nature. He is to collect the materials and analyse the same as per his experimental design.

People migrate from one geographical area to another and thereby are exposed to a different environmental condition. "By environment is here understood any condition, or group of conditions, external to the organism which may in anyway effect it. This includes such conditions as variations in temperature, humidity, barometric pressure, number and kinds of particles in the air, solar and cosmic radiation, food, water, mineral content of the soil, and all that is embraced under the terms social and economic condition" (Montagu, 1951 : 418). We have already referred to such situations where changes in bodily form took place primarily because of migration and change of environment. Those authors (Boas, Shapiro, Goldstein, etc.) fruitfully and meaningfully exploited those situations to derive scientific conclusions. In this connection we must not forget about the role of socio-economic conditions or the cultural factors in modifying the action of purely physical factors. We want to reemphasize here that human evolution should not be understood as a purely biological process and that biology and culture are two component parts of human evolution.

Northeast India with its geography and ethnic makeup is like a laboratory for anthropological research, where different theories could be tested and new ideas and thoughts be formulated and developed. We have already identified three population groups belonging to three different geographical regions—to study microevolutionary dynamics. There are many more areas and populations which can be explored from different angles.

Our populations are four divisions of the Khasi, four Boro populations and two sections of the Chutiyas. We have already established the fact that the ancestors of the Garos, Rabhas and Kacharis were originally the same and one people. Now each has its own socio-cultural and biological identity. We have stated that the Rajbanshis are the Hindu converts of those tribal populations. We have determined the base line and the end-product and also the intermediate stage. Again, we have found that the Khasis have four main divisions, namely, Khynriam, Pnar, Bhoi and War. Historical records reveal that the Deuris and the Chutiyas belong to the same parental population. Hence, it is justified to examine the microevolutionary dynamics in these three major populations.

We have already stated that in modern population genetics four basic factors, namely, mutation, selection, gene flow and genetic drift, are taken into consideration to explain differences in gene frequencies in human population groups or to understand human variation, both temporal and spatial.

Mutation does not appear to be a cause of variation among the present populations. The sizes of the populations are so large that it is difficult to visualize the role of genetic drift. However, this factor along with founder effect can not be completely ruled out because in the case of the Boro and Khasi it is difficult to ascertain when the tribal groups were formed, but perhaps long back. Besides, we do not know whether the splits took place at random or not.

We have demonstrated that ecological or environmental factors cause variation. The Plains Garos tend to deviate from the Hill Garos (Das, 1960). Differences are observed between the Plains Mālés and Hill Mālés (Sarkar, 1935-36). The Boro populations are met with in three different ecological conditions, namely, hilly habitat, sub-hilly region and river valley. Again, the populations are in three different stages of detribalization. Hence the populations are living in different environmental conditions. In the case of the Khasis also altitude varies from region to region where the different divisions live. The Bhois live in lower altitude. However, among the Chutiyas, no such differences in ecology or environment are observed as both the sections are met with in the river valley of the same geographical area.

Gene flow is another factor which deserves careful consideration. No doubt each of the populations is endogamous. The Deuris being the priestly section consider it as their moral obligation to preserve the traditional socio-cultural elements. They pay special attention not to marry outside the section, whereas the Chutiyas are a bit liberal in this matter. The formation of another section known as the Ahom-Chutiya confirms this supposition. Hence, perhaps gene flow is a very potent factor to cause microevolutionary dynamics in the case of the Deuris and Chutiyas.

The same process may be at work among the Bhois who do not live in complete isolation, as their territory is contiguous with that of populations other than the Khasis. Therefore, the possibility of infiltration of genes to the Bhois from the neighbouring populations can not be completely ignored. In the other divisions also, more particularly among the Khynriam and War, admixture with non-tribal caucasoid population has taken place. Though while collecting data we avoided these persons who were of mixed ancestry, but even then we can not say definitely that some genes have not entered unnoticed.

As regards the Boro populations, the Hill Garos live in considerable isolation. But the Kacharis and Rabhas have good contact with the other populations of that area. As a result exchange of genes between these populations might have taken place. The position of the Rajbanshis has already been explained.

On many occasions gene flows from one population to another unnoticed and in small numbers. Apparently this may not have any effect on the genetic makeup or biology of the population. But it has cumulative effect.

We have come across such phenomenon of slow flow of gene in small quantities from one population to another. The populations are not at all conscious about it. As an example we can refer to the Marias (a Muslim group) of Dibrugarh district of Assam. Haemoglobin E gene has entered into them from the neighbouriug populations, where the prevalence of this gene is very high (Das, 1977). In a similar manner the same gene has infiltrated to the Assamese Hindu castes from some mongoloid populations of Assam.

Thus, though we are not in a position to pin point a particular factor to be the cause of such microevolutionary trends, as a host of factors are involved in the process, yet we may perhaps put more stress on gene flow and environmental background.

So far we were mostly dealing with such populations which were originated because of migration and/or isolation. But admixture or fusion is also a potent factor for bringing about diversification. The hybrid group may be different from each of the parental populations and may form a distinct unit. In macro sense one does not come across such a population in Northeast India. At microlevel there are examples of emergence of such admixtured units, distinguishable from the ancestral groups.

In this connection perhaps we can recall the *New Theory of Human Evolution* of Sir Arthur Keith (1950). He has shown how in different parts of the world the numerous 'local groups' or 'tribes', due to various processes of detribalization, have united to form a nation. He has cited examples in support of his theory from all corners of the globe, specially from the Scots and the Egyptians. There were several local groups or tribes, each occupying its own territory, having its own administrations, laws, customs and manners, and keeping the tribal solidarity by way of isolation. Later on these tribal groups were amalgamated, gradually losing their local differences and became conscious of membership of a larger or national unit. With the process of detribalization of the tribes, the inborn predisposition and instinctive urges of the tribesmen, which owed allegiance to their chief or the administrative body and nursed the preferential interest of the tribe, became transferred to the wider circle of the nation. As local groups, which Keith calls 'evolutionary units' increased in size, passing from a tribal to a national stage, the power of assimilating fresh genes was practised in ever-widening circles, but the fresh genes incorporated were always from the same wide areas and of nearly the same genetic origin.

Nagaland, a State in Northeast India, is the homeland of the Nagas. The Naga is a sort of genetic name for a group of tribes, for example, Ao, Angami, Sema, Kabui, Konyak, Rengma, Lhota, Chang, etc. An analysis of the available anthropometric data (Das, 1970 : 4) reveals that the medium statured Angami are the tallest, while the short statured Kabui are the shortest of all. The Ao are also short statured people. The head form varies from dolichocephaly in the Ao, Chang, and Rengma to mesocephaly in the Angami, Sema, Lhota, Konyak and Kabui. The Angami, Ao, Chang, Sema and Rengma are mesorrhine,while the Konyak and Lhota are platyrrhine. The Kabui are leptorrhine. The face is broad in the Ao, while it is medium in the Kabui. Thus, the Nagas show a wide range of variation in morphological characters in the sense that nasal form varies from leptorrhiny in one group to platyrrhiny in the other; the head form also ranges from dolichocephaly to brachycephaly; the stature is also variable, suggesting heterogeneous nature of them. However, a genetic study is undoubtedly of utmost importance to testify the validity of the results obtained by analysis of the metric data.

Geographical condition of Nagaland and socio-cultural factors kept the different Naga populations in complete isolation for a long time. Various differentiating factors played their respective roles in different manners under different conditions resulting in physical variations among the Naga tribes. During the recent years because of political reasons, social movements and development projects, the barriers have gradually been lifted. Now the Nagas, in various senses, are forming one unit. It appears that each tribe of the Naga group is assimilating fresh genes, but the fresh genes incorporated are from the neighbouring areas and of nearly the same ethnic origin. Thus, a unification process appears to be on progress in Nagaland. One cannot, however, predict as regards what will be the genetic composition or biological status of the Nagas in future, but perhaps one can presume that if admixture among the tribes, after removal of geographical and socio-cultural barriers, continues freely, one day there may be one bigger Naga 'unit' in biological sense also. Here we can quote Keith, who is of opinion that "the people of Sweden are on the way to becoming a distinct variety of mankind" (Keith, 1950 : 328).

The Mataks of Upper Assam in ordinary sense form more a religious group than an ethnic one, because the group was originated on the basis of religion, though later on political forces also played part. But now they form a distinct group comprising people of mongoloid origin as well as of caste group. A study of cerumen type (Das, 1978) reveals that among the Matak neither the dry type nor wet type of cerumen is predominant, while in one of the ancestral groups, mongoloid, the dry type is very common, and in the other group, caste, the wet type is very frequent. Thus, in respect of gene frequencies of cerumen type at least, the Mataks have acquired a distinct characteristic, dissimilar from the ancestral populations.

In the beginning it was stated that the two principal aspects of physical anthropology are to study human evolution and variation. Evolution and variation are interlinked, as if they are the two faces of the same coin. But all variations may not be evolutionary in nature. To ascertain evolutionary dynamics one should find out variations between the ancestral and the descendant populations. In other words these two populations, that is, ancestral and descendant, are to be determined. It is not an easy task to find out where a population begins and where it ends. History of the populations may throw light on this problem. Then the biological aspects may be explored. Anyway, so far we were dealing with microevolutionary dynamics. Perhaps it will not be out of context if we now briefly refer to variation in biological characters among certain populations.

The Hindu castes are endogamous. They are also to some extent socially isolated. Therefore, the Hindu castes offer ample opportunity to study variation in man with regard to both social and physical aspects. Dobzhansky (1964 : 306) has rightly stated that "the castes of India are the most extreme example in recorded history of the retention of genetic differences between sympatric populations". Genetic and morphological variations among the castes and subcastes have great importance and are of much interest to the students of human evolution and variation. In Assam, however, casteism is not practised to that extent as is known in other states of India. This is perhaps, firstly, due to introduction of Vaisnavite cult by Srimanta Sankardeva, a socio-cultural reformer and a religious preacher of the 15th century; and secondly, Aryan influence came to Assam comparatively at a much later date. The Assamese caste-system is a bit different from that of other parts of India. The horizontal and vertical stratifications of the Assamese castes also tend to vary from that of other regions. But it is a fact that biological isolation because of prescribed mating system is very much there.

The Indian castes could be studied from various angles to arrive at conclusions of varied natures. In recent years some works on the castes of India have been done by some Indian scholars (Karve and Dandekar, 1951; Sanghvi and Khanolkar, 1949; Sanghvi, 1953; Malhotra, 1966; Gulati, 1968; Karve and Malhotra, 1968, etc.). For example, Sanghvi (1963) demonstrated biological differences among caste populations of Bombay. Different castes have striking different frequencies of ABO, Rh and MN blood groups as well as for taster ability and colour blindness. Karve and Malhotra (1968) have attempt to test Karve's hypothesis in biological sense.

While dealing with castes of India one should bear in mind that though a caste is taken as a Mendelian population, because of its endogamous character, yet certain castes are numerically so big and distributed over such a large geographical area that those fail to fulfil all the preconditions of a true Mendelian population. Theoretically, a person of a particular caste can marry any person of that caste, of course according to the prescribed marriage rules, but in practice sometimes it is seen that marriages are confined within members of particular geographical locality. Again, certain families of a caste prefer to select mates from families of particular lineages only. Thus, within the caste, selection and isolation may play parts even without necessarily giving rise to socially recognised subcastes. All these aspects deserve careful consideration when a caste is looked at from biological point of view.

Variations in certain biological characters among three Assamese castes, namely, Brahmin, Kalita and Kaibarta, were examined by the present author (Das, 1979). His study was based on the works reported earlier by him and his associates (Das, 1973, 1974, 1977; Das & Das, 1973, 1977; Das, Das & Das, 1973). In the caste hierarchy, the Brahmins occupy the highest position and the Kaibartas the lowest while the position of the Kalitas is in between the two. The Brahmins form the priestly caste. The Kalitas are scribes and agriculturists. The Kaibartas are fishermen and boatmen. Let us consider a few genetic traits as well as morphological characters of these three castes in order to ascertain their relative position bringing out biological variation among them.

Table 5.1 reveals that though gene B occurs in higher number than A in all the three castes, the difference between the two is more marked in the Kaibarta than in the other two. Gene A is more frequent in the Brahmin and Kalita than in Kaibarta. Therefore, the Kaibarta caste is significantly different from the Brahmin and Kalita, between which no significant differences are observed, as is revealed by the chi-square values.

TABLE 5.1: **Percentile frequencies of ABO blood groups and gene frequencies in the three castes**

Caste	N	O	A	B	AB	p	q	r
Brahmin	360	38.33	23.05	33.05	5.55	0.157	0.214	0.628
Kalita	454	38.54	24.22	31.29	5.94	0.165	0.208	0.626
Kaibarta	161	40.37	11.80	44.09	3.74	0.078	0.274	0.642

As regards cerumen type (Table 5.2), though in all the three castes the wet type is the dominant one, its frequency is very low in the Kaibarta (57.97%) in comparison to that in the Brahmin (70.59%) and Kalita (72.32%) Thus, the Kaibartas showing high number of dry cerumen tend to differ from the other two castes.

TABLE 5.2: **Percentile frequencies of cerumen type and gene frequencies in the three castes**

Caste	N	Wet type	Dry type	Gene frequency q(dry)
Brahmin	119	70.59	29.41	0.5423
Kalita	224	72.32	27.69	0.5261
Kaibarta	69	57.97	42.03	0.6483

As regards finger patterns (Table 5.3) in the Kaibartas whorl and loop occur almost in equal frequencies (50 : 50), whereas among the Brahmins and Kalitas the loop is much more frequent than whorl (60 : 40). Thus, the Kaibartas differ significantly from the Brahmin as well as Kalita as is found out by applying chi-square test.

TABLE 5.3: **Percentile frequencies of the three types of finger patterns in the three castes**

Caste	No	Whorl	Loop			Arch
			Radial	Ulnar	Total	
Brahmin	100	39.8	2.1	55.9	58.0	2.2
Kalita	100	40.0	1.9	53.9	55.6	4.2
Kaibarta	100	49.2	2.3	46.0	48.3	2.2

In respect of mean values cross section of head hair (Table 5.4) the three castes show significant variation from

TABLE 5.4: **Mean values of cross section of head hair in the three castes**

Caste	No. of person	No. of hairs	Maximum diameter Mean ±S.E. (micron)	Minimum diameter Mean ± S.E. (micron)
Brahmin	32	690	94.18±0.73	71.14±0.38
Kalita	48	970	97.37±0.61	72.93±0.41
Kaibarta	35	750	100.46±0.76	75.98±0.52

each other, as is revealed when *t*-test of significance is applied. It should be noted that the hair becomes coarser the more we descend in the caste hierarchy. The Kaibartas representing the low castes show the highest values for maximum and minimum diameters. These values decrease through the intermediate caste Kalita to toe highest caste Brahmin.

Seven anthropometric traits representing stature, head, face and nose were examined. The mean values (Table 5.5)

TABLE 5.5: Mean values of certain anthropometric traits in the three castes (males)

Measurements (in cm)	Brahmin (n=100) Mean±S.E.	Kalita (n=120) Mean±S.E.	Kaibarta (n=100) Mean ±S.E.
Stature	165.20±.53	163.63±.48	160.93±.64
Head length	18.63±.08	18.70±.05	18.49±.05
Head breadth	14.25±.05	14.55±.05	14.60±.05
Total facial height	11.32±.06	11.34±.05	11.11±.06
Maximum Bizygomatic breadth	13.11±.05	13.20±.05	13.26±.05
Nasal height	5.10±.03	5.03±.03	4.89±.03
Nasal breadth	3.49±.03	3.64±.02	3.72±.03
Indices			
Cephalic index	76.52±.37	77.87±.30	78.84±.30
Total facial index	85.86±.55	86.05±.52	85.45±.54
Nasal index	68.30±.63	72.67±.54	74.91±.78

and the values of *t*-test of significance (Table 6.6) suggest that in facial characters and head except head breadth, there are no significant differences among the three castes. But in respect of stature the Kaibartas are significantly shorter than the Brahmins as well as the Kalitas. Again, with regard to nasal index and also nasal breadth the Brahmins stand apart from the Kalita and Kaibarta.

TABLE 5.6: **Values of *t*-test of significance**

	Brahmin-Kalita	Brahmin-Kaibarta	Kalita-Kaibarta
Stature	2.19	5.14	3.37
Head length	0.74	1.48	3.00
Head breadth	4.28	5.00	0.71
Total facial height	0.03	2.50	2.94
Max. bizygomatic breadth	1.28	2.14	0.85
Nasal height	1.66	5.00	3.33
Nasal breadth	4.17	7.66	0.86
Cephalic index	2.83	2.77	2.28
Total facial index	0.25	0.53	1.06
Nasal index	5.27	6.59	2.32

In this connection it should be mentioned here that in a later study on bigger scale carried out by us in various castes of different geographical regions of Assam, we did not find biological variation among the castes exactly of the same nature and extent as was found in the earlier studies mentioned above. Different traits behaved in different manners in different regions in different castes. For example, as regards ABO blood groups A and B genes occur almost in equal frequencies in the low caste Hindu of Assam, whereas the high caste Assamese Hindu possess more B than A (Das *et al.*, 1978). However, there is no doubt that they showed variation confirming that populations, though of the same ethnic origin, tend to vary from each other in respect of biological traits because of various factors. We shall examine those materials while dealing with regional variation. Now let us have a discussion on the present materials on the three castes, namely, Brahmin, Kalita and Kaibarta.

We have found that with regard to ABO blood groups, cerumen type and finger patterns the Kaibartas stand apart from the Brahmins and Kalitas. The last two are very similar to one another. In this connection it may be mentioned that both the Brahmins and Kalitas belong to high caste group of the Hindus, while the Kaibartas represent a low caste, designated as a scheduled caste by the Government. Among the Kaibartas gene B is comparatively very high. In them dry type of cerumen occurs in a much higher percentage and whorl and loop type of finger patterns are found in the ratio of 1 : 1. By these they are different from the Brahmin and Kalita.

In respect of cross section of head hair and anthropometry no such picture is observed, but the data give us a different kind of indication. When the castes are arranged in a hierarcheal order, the hair becomes coarser from the Brahmin to the Kalita and then to the Kaibarta, as the mean values of maximum and minimum diameter increases from the higher caste to the lower one. A similar trend is observed as regards anthropometric traits. The stature shows a gradual increase from the Kaibarta to the Brahmin through the Kalita. From the low caste to the high caste head length shows an increase, while head breadth shows a decrease. As a result the head becomes longer and narrower as one proceeds from the lower to the higher caste. In the same manner nasal height increases and nasal breadth decreases from the Kaibarta to the Kalita and then to the Brahmin. As a consequence, the nasal index also decreases from the lower to the higher strata. In respect of face, however, no such definite trend is observed. But it may be pointed out that the Brahmins and Kalitas have slightly higher and narrower faces than the Kaibartas.

Now let us look at the possible explanation of the Kaibartas showing such a deviating tendency from the other two castes. Biological isolation may be one of the factors for such genetic variabilities. We have already come across similar phenomena among certain tribes of North East India, where subdivisions of the same tribe show such variations.

Then we must think of the possibility of gene flow to the castes from the neighbouring populations. In Assam the Caucasoid castes and Mongoloid tribes are living side by side for a very long time. Therefore, it is no wonder that exchange of genes between these two populations took place. In such a situation, mostly because of socio-cultural factors, the genes at first penetrate from the tribe to the lower strata of the caste. Then gradually a gene can find its way to the upper caste also.

Dry cerumen is considered to be a Mongoloid trait (Matsunaga 1962; Petrakis *et al.* 1967). The Mongoloid Populations of Northeast India exhibit dry cerumen in a very high percentage confirming the view of Matsunaga and others (Das, 1977). Among the Kaibartas dry cerumen occurs in 42.09%, whereas it is found in nearly 28% among the Brahmin and Kalita. Again, among the Kaibartas loop and whorl types of finger patterns occur in the ratio of 50 : 50. This ratio is considered to be a Mongoloid ratio. Further, the Mongoloid populations have coarser hair than the castes. All these suggest inflow of genes from the tribes to the Kaibartas.

The Brahmins came to Assam at a much later date and they are of Indo-Aryan stock. Different views have been expressed as regards the position of the Kalitas. But our results reveal that between the two Assamese high castes Brahmin and Kalita, there are no significant differenees in respect of physical traits.

Thus, for the possible explanation of variations in physical traits among the three castes, we are to think of several factors like ethnic migration, flow of genes, isolation.

As regards the trend in metric traits, we can perhaps add that Risley (1915) also observed that the higher the caste the finer is the nose. Buchi (1968) also noted a similar trend in the castes of South India. Though our data are inadequate, yet we also find a more or less similar trend in the Assamese castes.

The Assamese Muslims were also subjects of our study (Das, Das & Das, 1980). There are three broad sections of the Assamese Muslims, namely, the Sayeds, Sheikhs and Marias. The Sheikhs form the major bulk of the Assamese Muslim population. All of them belong to the Sunni sect of the Muslim community.

The Sheikhs and Marias were studied for four categories of physical anthropological variables. These are morphological traits (both somatoscopy and anthropometry), genetic traits (ABO blood groups and taste sensitivity to PTC), dermatoglyphic traits (finger patterns only) and behavioural traits (hand clasping, arm folding, handedness, dominant eye and tongue rolling).

The study reveals that in general the Marias differ from the Sheikhs in certain traits. The Marias are slightly different from the Sheikhs in head shape, face shape, etc., and also in certain observable characters. In behavioural traits also they appear to stand apart from the Sheikhs. In the occurrence of finger patterns also differences exist between the two groups. But in ABO blood groups and taste sensitivity no such differences are observed.

Now, how to account for such differences between these two sections of the Assamese Muslims ? It will be easier to find out the causes if we look at the historical records on the origin of these two sections and also examine the mating system. The available historical records reveal that the contemporary Assamese Muslim population includes three categories of people—one, the descendants of war prisoners who came to invade Assam under the leadership of several Mughal Generals; two, the immigrants who came occasionally in smaller numbers; and three, the local converts. Conversion usually took place through marriage.

The Muslim, first came to Assam in the early part of the thirteenth century. A Muslim General invaded Assam in 1206. The General lost the battle. It may be assumed that a few Muslim soldiers preferred to live in Assam instead of going back with their defeated leader. Since then, there were several Muslim invasions to Assam and every time the Muslims were defeated. Every time some Muslims were left behind in this part of the country. Thus, there were slow infiltrations of Muslims to Assam at different intervals of time. The descendants of these Muslims and the local converts are the Sheikhs of the present day.

There was another Muslim invasion in 1533 under the leadership of the Pathan General called Turbak. Turbak was defeated and killed. His soldiers were taken as prisoners and they were given settlement in different parts of Assam. These prisoners took to working in brass metal, the occupation which is still followed by many of their descendants. They are the Marias.

In the middle of the seventeenth century a Muslim saint came to Sibsagar district of Assam. He was a Sayed, but he married a local girl. The Assamese Sayeds mostly like to trace their ancestry from this saint.

Hence, we can trace back the origins of the three sections of the Assamese Muslims. The three sections evolved from three different sources. Then, we can look at the mating pattern. Though theoretically a Muslim can marry any Muslim, no doubt following the social norm, yet in practice marriages are confined to different sections. The Sayeds, who claim to be the descendants of prophet Hazarat Mohammed, prefer to take wives from the Sayed families. The Marias are regarded as having lower status in the Assamese Muslim society. Therefore, the Marias are to marry among themselves (Das, 1977). Thus, the three Muslim groups form three different endogamous groups in the broad sense. This has led to biological isolation which is a factor for biological variation.

Besides these two factors, historical background and endogamy, we can think of another aspect, and that is inflow of gene from the neighbouring populations. It has already been stated that local converts were added to the Muslim community. It has also been mentioned that the saint, the ancestor of the Sayeds, himself married a local girl, who was not a Muslim, but an Ahom. His example must have been followed by other Muslims of any of the sections. These informations definitely confirm that genes from other populations infiltrated into the Assamese Muslim population. This does not, however, mean that the identification of these three factors rules out the possibility of other factors responsible for causing variation.

Variation may be temporal or spatial. Now let us cast a glance on spatial variation. In studying spatial variation environment in which a population lives deserves special consideration. Environment may be geographical, cultural, ethnic and so on. Populations of the same ethnic origin living in different geographical regions appear to show variation in biological characters among them.

In discussing spatial or regional variations we shall take examples from Assam. The Assamese castes and the Assamese Muslim are distributed in different districts of the Brahmaputra valley of Assam. In collaboration with some of my colleagues a research project sponsored by the University Grants Commission, New Delhi, was recently completed (Das, Das & Das, 1980). In course of the investigation to the physical anthropology of certain population groups of Assam, we found that some population exhibit regional variation with regard to certain physical traits. Here we would like to cite a few cases only.

We shall take into consideration four populations, three of which are Assamese castes and the rest the Assamese Muslim. The castes are the Brahmin, Kalita and Kaibarta. The Brahmin samples come from three districts, namely, Kamrup, Darrang and Sibsagar, while the Kalita samples have been drawn from five districts, namely, Goalpara, Kamrup, Nowgong, Darrang and Sibsagar. The Kaibarta samples are from Goalpara, Darrang, Nowgong, Kamrup and Dibrugarh; and the Muslim samples from Goalpara, Kamrup, Darrang, Nowgong and Sibsagar (please refer to Map No. 2). Though in the research project several physical anthropological traits were included, here we shall take into account certain metric traits, ABO blood groups, taste sensitivity to PTC and finger patterns.

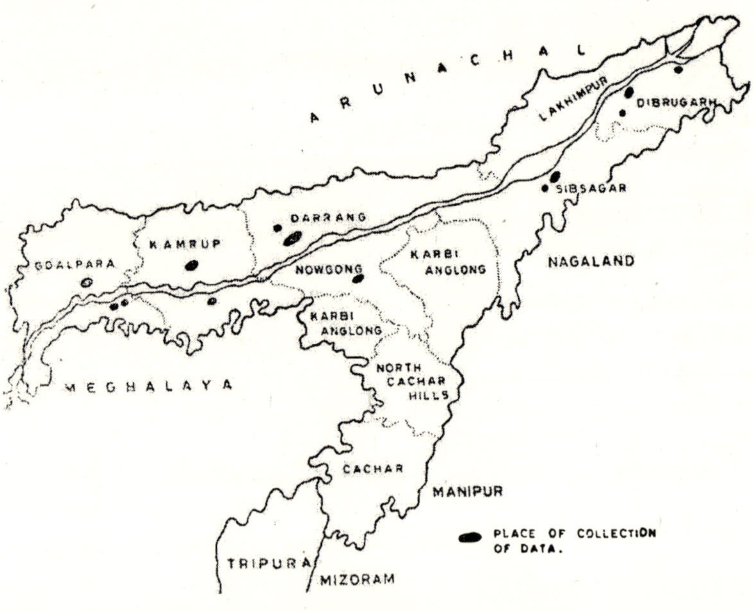

Map 2: Sketch Map of Assam

For the purpose of comparison among the samples of the different districts, depending upon the nature of data, either *t*-test of significance or chi-square test was applied. Again, to measure morphological distances and genetical distances between the districts Sanghvi's (1953) T^2-method and G-test were used.

Brahmin

The Kamrup Brahmins differ from the Darrang Brahmins in 7 and from the Sibsagar Brahmins in 4, and the Darrang Brahmins from the Sibsagar Brahmins in 3 out of 12 metric traits. Thus, the Sibsagar Brahmins are more similar to the Kamrup as well as Darrang Brahmins, than the Kamrup and Darrang Brahmins. This observation is based on the values of *t*-test of significance. The values of T^2-method also reveal a similar picture.

With regard to ABO blood groups there are no statistically significant differences among the three Brahmin samples. In respect of occurrence of tasters and non-tasters the Darrang Brahmins are significantly different from each of the Kamrup and Sibsagar Brahmins. However, mean threshold does not reveal significant difference among the three Brahmin samples. With regard to dermatoglyphic traits a wide range of variation is observed among the Brahmins.

Thus, the Assamese Brahmins show regional variation to a considerable extent. But similarities and dissimilarities among the Brahmins of the three regions do not show a single uniform trend with regard to different types of variable.

Kalita

A careful scrutiny of the Kalita samples from five different districts reveals considerable amount of biological variation. Of the metric traits, nose form and face form appear to be more variable. The head form also varies to a considerable extent. But stature does not vary much. Variation is observed with regard to two genetic traits—ABO blood groups and taste sensitivity to PTC. However, in respect of dermatoglyphic traits inter-district variability appears to be less in comparison to other traits.

Kaibarta

Inter-district variability is negligible in respect of dermatoglyphic traits. As regards number of taster and non-taster persons among the Kaibartas of different districts, inter-district differences are not significant almost in all the cases. However, mean threshold shows variation. In ABO blood group frequencies the Kaibartas of Dibrugarh district stand apart from those of other districts. Otherwise, inter-district variations are not noteworthy.

With regard to metric characters inter-district variation is more than that in dermatoglyphic and genetic traits. The Kaibartas of Darrang, Nowgong and Dibrugarh district form a cluster, being very similar to each other, whereas the Kaibartas of Goalpara and Kamrup districts stand quite apart from one another and at the same time from those of the other three districts.

Muslim

The study reveals that among the Muslims (Sheikh) inter-district biological variations are considerably high. Of the metric traits face and nose show comparatively more variability than head and stature. The greatest amount of variation is observed in respect of ABO blood groups. The same is true with regard to finger patterns also. As regards occurrence of taster and non-taster individuals inter-district variation is comparatively less, but mean threshold show a wide range of variation.

The studies give several important information. The amount of inter-district variability is not the same in all the populations. Among the Kaibartas variation is almost negligible. The opposite picture is observed among the Muslims and the Kalita. The Brahmins stand in between these two extremes. Again, different variables behave in different manners in different populations. No uniform trend is observed. But the facts remain that regional variations among the people of the same group exist. However, this is a known fact.

At the present state of our knowledge it is very difficult to offer a definite explanation for such nature and extent of spatial variation in the Assamese Hindu castes and Assamese Muslims. We have already noted earlier that differences in ecological factors may lead to biological variation. In the present context geographical environment is more or less the same. All the districts lie in the Brahmaputra valley. However, ethnic environment varies to a certain extent from region to region. The possibilities of inflow of genes from the neighbouring populations to those Hindu castes and Muslims causing variation can not be totally ruled out. But for proper estimation of this situation we must have comparative data from these surrounding populations of each of the districts, which we do not have at the moment.

Another fact deserves consideration. All the samples come from rural areas. It was found that most of the marriages were confined to a particular region. The people preferred to marry from the nearby villages. Hence, each sample represents one particular region. There are examples to demonstrate that.

Long continued intermarriage in comparatively isolated population leads to formation of district biological identity. Can we think of functioning of this type process causing inter-district variation ?

As regards the Muslims another factor may be added. We have already mentioned earlier that many of the Assamese Muslims are local converts. Therefore, if the local populations vary from region to region, then the Muslims who include local converts should show regional variation. As a matter of fact such phenomenon was observed by us (Das & Deka, 1980) in respect of occurrence of abnormal haemoglobin E among the Rajbanshis, who were originally tribal people. The Rajbanshis of different regions are very similar to their respective ancestral groups.

The sample size also undoubtedly produced some of the variations among populations of different regions.

Thus, it appears that several factors are involved in producing regional variation among the members of the same population; whatever might be the reasons, the fact remains that the Assamese castes and Muslims show inter-district biological variation to a considerable extent.

Advances both in theory and in the accumulation of information through different kinds of researches in the biological sciences, including anthropology, have helped us to understand the trends of evolution; the process by which genetic materials are distributed within populations; and how new varieties of populations can emerge. The possibilities of genetic diversity, which exist within the human species are enormous.

Innovation of modern techniques of studying the nature and behaviour of genes and advancement of mathematical genetics have equipped the physical anthropologists to explore the new facts of human evolution opening up a new era in anthropology. The fact that evolution is directed by the interaction between cultural components and genetic materials has encouraged collaboration between cultural and physical anthropologists at a research level.

In fine we can say that it is an established fact that mankind evolved. It is demonstrable that mankind is evolving. It is presumable that mankind will continue to evolve.

Bibliography

Allen, B.C., *Assam District Gazetters*, 3, Goalpara, 1905.

Basu, A., Namboodiri, K.K., Weitkamp, L.R., Brown, W.H., Pollitzar, W.S. and Spirvey, M.A. Morphology, Serology, Dermatoglyphics and Microevolution in some village population in Haiti, West Indies, *Human Biology*, 48 (2), 1976, pp. 245-269.

Buchi, E.C., Caste and race in south India, *The Anthropologist*, Spec. Vol., 1968, pp. 61-67.

Boas, F., *Changes in Bodily Form of Descendants of Immigrants*, Washington, D.C., 1911.

Boyd, W.C., *Genetics and the Races of Man*, Oxford : Blackwell Scientific Publication, 1950.

Buettner-Janusch, J., *Origins of Man*, Bombay : Wiley Eastern Private Limited, 1969.

Dalton, E.T., *Descriptive Ethnology of Bengal*, Calcutta : 1872.

Das, B.M., Somatic variations among the Hills and plains Garo of Assam, *Man in India*, 49 (2), 1960, pp. 128-148.

Das, B.M., Somatic variability among some populations of south Goalpara, Assam, *Proc. Nat. Inst. Sc. India*, 30 B (5 & 6), 1964, pp. 315-338.

Das, B.M., Somatic variability in south Goalpara, Assam, *Acta Genet. Med Gemell*, 16 (2), 1967, pp. 178-189.

Das, B.M., *Anthropometry of the Tribal Groups of Assam, India*, Miami: Field Research Projects, 1970.

Das, B.M., Caste and head hair, *Indian Anthropologist*, 3, 1973, pp. 135-138.

Das, B.M., A study of cross section of head hair from some caucasoid and mongoloid populations of Assam, India, *Z. Morph. Anthrop.*, 65 (3), 1974, pp. 324-328.

Das, B.M., Trend of variation in respect of certain anthropometric traits in two populations of northeast India, *Seminar on Human Variation in India*, Anth. Surv. India, 1977.

Das, B.M., Inheritance of cerumen type and its importance in population study, *Man in India*, 57 (4), 1977, pp. 305-312.

Das, B.M., Inheritance of cerumen type and its importance in population studies, *Man in India*, 57, 1977, pp. 305-312.

Das, B.M., Cerumen types in some populations of northeast India, *The Anthropologist*, 13 (1 & 2), 1975 & 1978, pp. 30-36.

Das, B.M., *Variation in Physical Characteristics in the Khasi Population of North East India*, Gauhati : Dutta Barua & Co., 1978.

Das, B.M., On some aspects of variation and ongoing human evolution, Presidential address, Section of Anth. Arch. 66th Ind. Sc. Cong. Assoc. Hyderabad, *Man in India*, 59, 1978, 1: 1—25, 1979.

Das, B.M., Physical variation in three Assamese castes, *Anthrop. Anz. Jg*., 37 (3), 1979, pp. 204-210.

Das, B.M. and Das, P.B., Distances anthropometriques entre quarte castes de L' Assam, Inde. *L' Anthropologie*, 77 (5-6), pp. 637-643.

Das, B.M. and Das, P.B., Frequency of colour blindness in five groups of Assam, *Man in India*, 53 (4), 1973, pp. 363-367.

Das, B.M., Variation among four Assamese castes in respect of finger patterns, Abs. in *Proc. Ethn. & Folk Cul. Soc. & Ind. As. Phy. Anth*., 1977.

Das, B.M., Deka, R. and Das, R., Haemoglobin E in six populations of Assam, *Jr. Ind. Anth. Soc*., 15 (2), 1980.

Das, B.M., Das, P.B. and Das, R., Genetic distances in respect of ABO blood groups among four castes of Assam, India, *Humangenetik*, 20, 1973, pp. 179-181.

Das, B.M., Das, P.B. and Das R., Population and regionwise variation in the distribution of ABO blood groups in Assam, India, *Abs. No. 0051, Vol. I, Xth ICAES*, New Delhi, 1978.

Das, B.M. Das, P.B. and Das, R., *The Assamese Muslims : Their Physical Features*, Study No. 6, UGC sponsored scheme, Anth. Dept., Gauhati University, 1980.

Das, B.M., Das P.B. and Das, R., *Variation in Physical Characteristics in the Kaibartas of Assam*, Study No. 5, UGC sponsored scheme, Anth. Dept., Gauhati University, 1980.

Das, B.M., Das, P.B. and Das, R., *Biological variation in the Kalita : A caste of Assam*, Study No. 4, UGC sponsored scheme, Anth. Dept., Gauhati University, 1980.

Das, B.M., Das, P.B. and Das, R., *Physical Anthropology of the Brahmins of Assam*, Study No. 3, UGC sponsored scheme, Anth. Dept., Gauhati University, 1980.

Das, F.A., A study of genetic composition of the Assamese Muslims of Dibrugarh (Assam), Unpublished Ph.D. Thesis of Dibrugarh University, 1977.

Dobzhansky, T., *Genetics and the Origin of Species*, Kharagpur: Oxford University Press, 1964.

Goldstein, M., *Demographic and Bodily Changes in the Descendants of Mexican Immigrants*, Inst. of Latin-American Studies, University of California, 1943.

Greulich, W.W., A comparison of physical growth and development of America-born and native Japanese children, *Am. J. Phys. Anthrop.*, n.s., 15, 1957, pp. 489-516.

Guiati, R.K., *Intergroup differences in An Artisan Caste of Maharastra*, Miami : Field Research Projects, 1971.

Hirszfeld, L. and Hirszfeld, H., Serological difference between the blood of different races, *Lancet*, 197, 1919, pp. 675-679.

Hulse, F.S., Adaptation, selection, and plasticity in ongoing human evolution, *The Progress on Ongoing Human Evolution* (ed. Laskar, G.W.), Detroit : Wayne State University Press, 1960.

Hulse, F.S., Some factors influencing the relative proportions of human racial stocks, Cold Spring Harbor Symposium, Quant. Bio., 22, 1957, pp. 33-45.

Ito, P.K., Anthropometric study of new-born infants of Japanese parents in America, *Am. J. Dis. Child*, 52, 1936, 321-330.

Karve, I. and Dandekar, V.M., *Anthropometric Measurements of Maharastra*, Deccan College Monograph series 8, Poona, 1951.

Karve, I. and Malhotra, K.C., A biological comparison of eight endogamous groups of the same rank, *Current Anthropology*, 9, 1963, pp. 109-124.

Keith, A. 1950, *A New Theory of Human Evolution*, London : Watts & Co., 1950.

Kraus, B.S. and White, C.B., Microevolution in a human population : A study of social endogamy and blood type distribution among the Western Apache, *Amer. Anth.*, 58 (6), 1956, pp. 1017-1043.

Laskar, G.W., Migration and physical differentiation : A comparison of immigrants with American-born Chinese, *Am. J. Phys. Anthrop.*, n.s. 4, 1946, pp. 273-300.

Laskar, G.W., Environmental growth factors and selective migration, *Human Biology*, 24, 1952, pp. 262-289.

Laskar, G.W., The question of physical selection of Mexican migrants of the U.S.A., *Human Biology*, 26, 1954, pp. 52-57.

Malhotra, K.C., Anthropometric measurements and blood groups of Maharastra Brahmins, Unpublished Ph. D. Thesis, Poona University, Poona, 1966.

Malhotra, K.C., Microevolutionary dynamics among the Gavdas of Goa, *Evolutionary Models and Studies in Human Diversity*, Eds. R.J. Meier, C.M. Otten and F.A. Hameed, The Hague : Mouton, 1978, pp. 280-314.

Matsunaga, E., The diamorphism in human normal cerumen, *Ann. Hum. Gen*, 25, 1962, pp. 273-285.

Motulsky, A.G., Metabolic Polymorphisms and the role of Infectious Diseases in Human Evolution, *The Progress of Ongoing Human Evolution*, Ed. W.G. Laskar, Detroit : Wyane State University Press, 1960.

Montagu, M.F.A., *An Introduction to Physical Anthropology*, Illinois: 1951.

Oliver, D.L. and Howells, W.W., Microevolution : Cultural elements in physical variation, *Amer. Anth.*, 59 (6), 1957, pp. 965-978.

Petrakis, N.L., Molohon, K.T. & Tepper, D.J., Cerumen in American Indians : Genetic implication of sticky and dry types, *Science*, 158, 1967, pp. 1192-1193.

Risley, H., *The People of India*, Calcutta : 1915.

Sanghvi, D.L. and Khanolkar, V.R., Data relating to seven genetical characters in endogamous groups in Bombay, *Ann. Eugenics* 15, 1949, pp. 52-64.

Sanghvi, L.D., Comparison of genetical and morphological methods for a study of biological differences, *Am. J. Phys. Anthrop.*, 11, 1953, pp. 385-404.

Sarkar, S.S., The racial affinities of the inhabitants of the Rajmahal Hills, *Trans. Bose Res. Ins.*, 11, 1935-36, p. 123.

Sarkar, S.S., Race and race movements in India, *Cultural Heritage of India*, Calcutta, 1, 1958.

Shapiro, H.L., *Migration and Environment*, New York : Oxford University Press, 1939.

Spier, L., Growth of Japanese children born in America and in Japan, *Univ. Washington Pub. Anthropol.* 3, 1929.

Spuhler, J.N. and Kluckhohn, C., Inbreeding coefficients of the Ramah Navaho population, *Human biology*, 25, 1953, pp. 295-317.

Tax, S., *The Celebration, a Personal View On Evolution after Darwin 3*, Chicago : University of Chicago Press, 1960.

Wallas, B. and Dobzhansky, T., Genes in Mendelian population, *Human Evolution*, Ed. N. Korn and F. Thompson, London, Holt. Rinehart and Winston, Inc., 1967.

Waddell, L.A., The tribes of the Brahmaputra valley, *Jr. As. Soc. Beng.*, 69 (3), 1901.

INDEX